To my family,
those who came before
those who are here now
and those who are to come

Augusta Elizabeth Fox Vesecky

WATERMELON DREAMS

A Legacy

AUSTIN MACAULEY PUBLISHERS™

LONDON • CAMBRIDGE • NEW YORK • SHARJAH

Ordering Information
Quantity sales: Special discounts are available on quantity purchases by corporations, associations, and others. For details, contact the publisher at the address below.

Publisher's Cataloging-in-Publication data
Vesecky, Augusta Elizabeth Fox
Watermelon Dreams

ISBN 9781645750895 (Paperback)
ISBN 9781645750901 (ePub e-book)

www.austinmacauley.com/us

Library of Congress Control Number: 2021918375

First Published 2021
Austin Macauley Publishers LLC
40 Wall Street, 33rd Floor, Suite 3302
New York, NY 10005
USA

mail-usa@austinmacauley.com
+1 (646) 5125767

I am indebted to my family for stories shared over the years, especially to my mother, Fern Vesecky Fox; my father, Donald Jay Fox; my aunts, Ruth Minter and Eva Kathary, who just recently passed away – the last of her generation in my family; my uncle, Bill Larson, whose handwritten memoir of my Vesecky grandparents' years in Kansas City contributed to the narrative.

Throughout the writing of this book, I have been inspired by all the people in my family, but I want to acknowledge those who have gone before – my parents and grandparents, all my aunts and uncles, as well as several cousins: David Cooney, Steve Minter, Susan Emrich, Hugh Emrich, Stephanie Vesecky and Christy Larson.

I also wish to honor my brother, Frank; my daughter, Kirsten; my son, Brendan; and especially my sister, Katy, who was born too late to have been a part of these early memories, and who died too soon to witness their fruition.

"…the story is all that we have when things are over
the story begins as an echo of what went before
but then it is only the story we are listening to."
from *The Folding Cliffs*
– W. S. Merwin

*The afternoon sun beat down on her shoulders,
as she slowly drove the cows home for milking.
Her old mare's back was warm and sweaty
beneath her, and the hot bugs of summer
droned slower and slower…until she slipped
to the ground. Still half asleep, she clambered
back on the patient old horse, standing still
for her in the hot summer sun, lazily flicking
the flies off her rump with a brush of her tail.*

My mother, Fern Vesecky, was born March 8, 1913, on a farm near a tiny Czech town, in west-central Kansas. The farm was on the other side of Walnut Creek, about a half-mile or so from Timken, named for Henry H. Timken, an inventor and land speculator who insisted the town be named after him when he sold the land to the Railroad Town Site Company. (See "Legends of Kansas: History, Tales and Destinations in the land of Ahs"). My grandparents were proud of this farm, which, in addition to a full-sized barn, chicken house and other outbuildings, featured a modern Sears Roebuck frame house with a small parlor, four bedrooms, dining room, kitchen with a wood stove that was later converted to gas, and an indoor bathroom, complete with lavatory, toilet and claw foot tub—the latter becoming rust-stained over the years by the iron in well water, drawn by a pump and one-time working windmill in the back yard.

The third child of Czech immigrant parents, my mother was four and two years younger than her brothers Albert and Stephen respectively—and the baby of the family until her sister Marie came along and "took all the attention," as my mother used to say. From being 'Little Fern' or 'Fernie,' she became just Fern—and relinquished the favored baby spot to Marie, who my mother thought was cuter than she. Marie had big brown eyes and dark hair, a sweet round face and small, doll-like body. My mother, in fact, was the *only* child of the four who had greenish-brown eyes, red hair, long limbs and the freckles she carried throughout much of her life. In her own mind, she was the ugly duckling, and though she grew to be a 'swan,' and strove to succeed, I think she never got over her feelings of inferiority.

As the elder daughter, she was given more of the farm chores. Besides herding cows and helping with the housework, she looked after Marie and was the designated companion of her cranky, ornery, maternal grandmother, who was failing in health and blamed everyone else, including my mother, for it. When the grouchy, mean grandmother died, my mother was both relieved, and horrified, by the grotesque sight of her corpse sprawled in a chair, her mouth gaping and her dead eyes wide open. It was this great-grandmother who filled my grandmother's Christmas stocking with cow chips one year because she was 'bad'.

As for my mother's life as a cowgirl, it was anything but romantic, and she vowed early on that she would never marry a farmer. Perhaps it was the barnyard smells of horse manure and chicken droppings. Perhaps it was the indoor, nearly suffocating, stench of freshly killed chickens soaking in boiled water, waiting to be plucked. Perhaps it was the dream of being something other than a second-generation Czech and having the need to prove herself. At any rate, my mother never harbored the nostalgia for the farm that was to be my inheritance.

For me, the modest acreage held by my grandparents offered a landscape of rippling wheat fields I thought of as ocean waves many years before I even glimpsed the sea — and of corn stocks so high I could hide in their rustling midst. It offered sensuous memories of sliding between crisp muslin sheets, laundered with homemade soap, and sun-dried to an inimitable freshness. And it was the farmhouse itself, so different from my Wichita suburban childhood homes, that became *the* home place to which over the years, I have returned in dreams, as though trying to recapture, reclaim it as mine.

Though the farm supplied the family with chickens, geese, ducks and eggs, along with veggies from Grandma Lizzie's garden — and money from the rented fields — it was off and on over the years only part-time employment for my grandfather, John Vesecky. Born May 13, 1879, he had entered the country with his family as an infant from a province called Czechy in Bohemia, then a part of the Austro-

Hungarian empire, which became Czechoslovakia for a brief period between the wars, and which now is part of the modern-day Czech Republic. My grandfather became a student, then a teacher, then while farming, a populist supporter of farm cooperatives. Later as president of the National Farmers Union, he gave a speech which tells his story (Appendix I), as well as a New Year's radio address to the National Farmers Union in 1939 (Appendix II).

For my grandmother, born Elizabeth Kraisinger, April 14, 1886, the farm was a full-time job. Born in the U.S. of Czech immigrants, she threw herself into farm life with all the inherited strength and vitality from her parents, who had come from the Sudetenland bordering Germany (hence her Germanic, rather than typically Slavic, name).

I sometimes wondered whether Grandma loved her children nearly as much as her chickens. I often watched her clucking to them as she threw out handfuls of table scraps on which they descended as though starved, fighting over the choice items. On the glass doors separating the entrance hall from the dining room of their farm house, she had pasted cut-outs of exotic fowl, some of which she had tried to raise herself, until the ordinary hens pecked them nearly to death out of jealousy.

Of course, Grandma had no hesitation in grabbing, beheading and dressing her hens for the family dinner. There was a bloodied table underneath a black walnut tree where she swung her ax and flung the hapless, headless chickens on the grass to flop and bleed. I often liked to perch in this tree while reading a book, and I had to stand atop the table in order to climb the tree. It was this same gruesome table that I leapt on once while fleeing a nasty rooster, who had chased me first around the barnyard. It was Uncle Al, my mother's brother, who laughingly rescued me. My embarrassment was lessened by the knowledge that the same nasty rooster had chased many others besides me — and subsequently ended up under the ax.

Yet, Grandma's chickens rewarded her with baby chicks and fine eggs, which she traded for milk products from her sister's dairy farm not far away. Great-aunt Katy Smrka, with her husband Bill, lived on a farm closer to town and supplied my grandparents with butter, cream and whole milk, while Lizzie offered her the best eggs, fresh chickens and ducks or geese for the Christmas table. We kids were rather frightened of rough Aunt Katy, even more than Great-uncle Bill. My mother always said that she was 'a beauty' when young, but we had a great deal of difficulty visualizing her whiskered chin, toothless grin and stringy grey hair (always covered by a kerchief cap) as belonging to a 'beauty.'

My grandmother also kept a handsome garden bordered by her favorite multi-colored zinnias, and each summer she put up quarts of tomatoes, 'chow-

chow' relish, green beans, peas, sweet pickles and endless jars of her favorite, ground horseradish, which she used to stuff into our family cars as we were driving away after a visit. Since these were quart jars, we never seemed to finish one before another was urged upon us. We ate a lot of horseradish.

While visiting the farm with my younger brother Frank, I often tried to help my grandmother with the harvesting and weeding, but my allergies sent me wheezing and sneezing to the walnut tree with my books, followed by Grandma's disdainful Czech upbraiding. Potatoes, onions, and turnips she stored in the backyard root cellar, that doubled as a storm cellar, into which the family would descend when our grandfather, self-made storm watcher, ordered everyone through wind-whipped nights to wait out furious storms. The cellar door was made of tin, so that sounds of the raging weather outside were amplified to terrifying decibels.

Neither of my Vesecky grandparents was large of stature—but both were strong, sturdy hard workers. My grandfather, Grandpa John, wore thick glasses that made his eyes appear larger. Both these, and his gruff voice and blunt manner, used to frighten me as a young child, but became endearing to me as I grew older. His clothes never seemed to fit properly. His belt, for instance, cinched his waist which was smaller than the trousers he wore, and his shoes were black and well-worn.

Grandma Lizzie, though a redhead when young, had the same color of charcoal and grey hair, which she wore in a severe middle part. Her long braids were coiled at the back of her head, neatly out of the way for doing unending chores. She had a set of bone grooming accessories she kept on her dresser, and I used to like looking at myself in the hand mirror and smelling her comb and brush that always had her particular scent—neither pleasant nor unpleasant but faintly oily, since she rarely washed her long hair. She wore cotton dresses with crisp white collars, and sometimes she fastened a brooch in the center. She too wore the plain black shoes—usually laced or button-up high tops, and she always wore coarse stockings. Her speech was sprinkled with Czech slang and colloquialisms, more so than my grandfather's, and she sometimes used these to keep me from hearing her often ribald jokes. She never excelled in school, and wrote clumsily in her own phonetic script. Lizzie and John married—after my grandfather, then Lizzie's teacher, gave up trying to tame this wild girl at whom he once threw a blackboard eraser—and after she decided, since she wasn't a good student, she would just "marry the teacher." These two people became as parents to me during the war years, and I came to love their stern tenderness.

My mother, as I have said, continued to grow up hating farming. She defended herself against the sometimes-cruel pranks played on her by her older brothers, who once managed to light a fire in her toy stove, burning it up. They teased her unmercifully, and only later in their adult life did she and all her siblings become good friends and loyal supporters of one another, gathering together for warm and rollicking Christmases at the farm.

II

While my mother was bemoaning her chore-laden farm life, my father was living a charmed existence in a town not far away. Born April 25, 1912, in the small farming community of Longford, Donald Jay Fox was my paternal grandparents' first child after 10 years of marriage, and he was lucky enough to be the only boy of five children. His parents were Franklin Daniel Fox and Cora Katherine George, who met and courted while attending Salina Normal College. (See Appendix III for an episode of Frank and Cora's courtship). Not much is known about my paternal ancestors; over several generations, they emigrated from England, Sweden, and Germany, many of them settling in Pennsylvania. My father referred to them as "Pennsylvania Dutch." There is an element of mystery about these ancestors, and my father and aunts all have mentioned secret whisperings in the parlor about the family's history. I have often wondered just what kind of secret they harbored: *Were we part Jewish? Had there been an illegitimate birth? Did we actually have*

Gypsy blood? For my part, I secretly wished for some exotic genetic mix contributing to our family tree.

A seemingly childless couple, Grandma and Grandpa Fox were overjoyed to at last have a son, whose infant beauty and goodness so amazed them that they were unable to even give him a name for several weeks after his birth. In a diary kept by my grandfather—with a few entries by my grandmother—he refers to the simple joys of parenthood in understatements that belie their adoration: "Boy grows healthy and strong," and later, "Donald is teething…" etc.

They soon embraced their new life as parents, as well as each other, for every two years, my grandmother gave birth to a daughter—four in all, named Genevieve Elizabeth, Ruth Maurine, Mary Maxine and Eva Jean (affectionately called 'Babe' by my father). But he seemed always the favored child, "born with a silver spoon in his mouth," my mother used to remark, somewhat bitterly. He was always the first to bathe in the single portable bathtub, filled with hot water, in the kitchen. *Then* his sisters and parents would follow. Strangely enough, Eva, though the baby, was always last. Then my grandfather would line them all up, cut their hair and trim their finger and toe nails.

Donald was fussed over and given unusual gifts. One Christmas, my grandfather scoured the countryside to come up with a goat my father pined for — a dairy goat with a milk stand and a little cart in which the adored boy could drive his goat around town, the envy of his sisters and playmates. Apparently, he milked the goat just once and soon tired of the novelty *and* the responsibility. Years later, it was a pool table he wanted, then a miniature golf 'course.'

Actually, my grandfather spoiled all his children. One Christmas, Eva pined for a canary in a cage, so my grandfather went out and found one for her. At another time, Eva became 'Mom' to three geese, who imprinted on her, following her around. She lost her flock, though, when they became the main dish for the family table.

The ultimate gift for my father, of course, was a car. My aunt Genevieve wrote about this car (a Ford, of course), and the envy it produced, in a school assignment, a charming journal in which she describes stealing my father's car — no matter that she didn't know how to drive — and taking it on a joyride with a girlfriend, ending up in a harmless crash that nevertheless damaged the prized possession *and*, at least temporarily, the brother-sister relationship (see Appendix IV).

My father and Aunt Genevieve resembled each other the most of the five children. Both had wavy hair (his was the color of honey, while hers was nearly black) and lovely ice-blue eyes. The other sisters were all blond and blue-eyed and bonded together as a trio, as they continued to do in their later years, my Aunt Ruth taking charge. "She always does," my father once said.

Another mishap with a car happened when my father was an infant, being taken on an outing in the family car, a Model T. He was being tended to by some aunts, and when the car stalled on a hill, they all panicked and jumped out, leaving my father sitting placidly in the back seat, enjoying the downhill adventure that ended with the car lodging harmlessly in a ditch.

The family was fairly well off as rural families go, my grandfather running a successful general store business in Longford, farming and later turning to car dealership and gas stations in nearby Salina. (As youngsters, my cousins and I liked to loiter around Grandpa's Mobil Oil station, dropping coins into the peanut and bubble gum vendor machines, smugly sipping free pop). The family always took a summer vacation together, motoring to Colorado, the 'Shangri-La' of Kansans, camping along the way. Cora would fry up several chickens and make potato salads—to last the trip!

"Didn't you all get sick?" we asked, listening to the nostalgic reminiscence of my father about these trips.

"Sick as dogs!" he snorted.

One late departure once forced them to camp after dark. After driving around for a while, my grandfather set up the tent in the middle of a nice grassy area he thought suitable. It wasn't until morning that they discovered they were camped in the middle of a courthouse lawn—much to the amusement of the townspeople.

My father's parents and siblings were also fond of picnicking. On one such occasion many years later, my cousins and I were held in rapt attention by Grandpa Fox's storytelling. Awaiting with impatience the first sweet watermelon of the season, we gathered around Grandpa Fox as he cut into a green-striped giant of a melon and distributed generous wedges to the thirsty, sweaty throng around him. And this thirsty, sweaty throng, sitting cross-legged, plunging teeth first into deep pink luscious slices, made a captive audience for Grandpa's stories. This is how I remember it:

One midsummer Kansas night, when Grandpa was far from being a grandpa—about the age of 14—and when the full moon was throwing wild shadows over the usually familiar farm landscape, Grandpa, whose name was Franklin Daniel, awoke to an urgent voice calling up to him from below his bedroom window.

"Frank, Frank!" the voice called. "Wake up and come outside!"

Sleepily, Frank dragged himself out of bed and over to the window, and not seeing anyone below—only the long shadows the moon made on the farm house lawn—was about to crawl back into bed, when the voice repeated, "Come outside!"

So Frank, using a trick he had read about, lowered himself from his window with his bed sheets tied together, not wishing to disturb his sleeping family, and of course, now quite curious about this voice that sounded so insistent and this person who knew his name.

When he reached the grass below and still was unable to see the person who had called to him, he noticed that the chickens—which usually at this time of night would be asleep on their roost, dreaming chicken dreams and making the eggs for his breakfast—were awake and out in the barnyard, racing around distractedly. And the horses, too, seemed restless in their stalls and whinnied nervously.

Rather than crawl back into his bedroom window and try to go back to sleep (for Frank was wide awake by now and ready for adventure), he took one of the horses out of its stall, mounted it and rode off in the moonlight toward a neighboring farm, thinking perhaps it was his friend Ned who had called him and then, to play a joke, had disappeared.

Thence began a mad chase about the countryside, riding from farm to farm, looking for the phantom voice. At one farm, Frank threw pebbles up to what he thought was a friend's window, when someone he did not know opened the window, aimed a rifle at him—and fired!

This resounding *crack!* (fortunately, a misfire, or else Grandpa would not have been telling this story and we would not have been there to hear it), shocked some sense into Frank, and he hastily retreated, galloping frantically all the way back to his own farmyard. He put his panting, sweaty horse back into its stall, climbed the knotted bed sheets into his window and fell, exhausted, into bed.

The next morning after chores, while eating the fresh eggs at breakfast, Frank was reminded of the chickens running in the moonlight, the restless horses and the mysterious voice which had called to him—and had nearly got him killed. He told his story to his mother, who smiled knowingly, as mothers do, and said, "Why son, you ate too much watermelon last night before you went to bed. You had a watermelon dream!"

Well, Frank—that is, Grandpa Fox—told this story many times to us kids, always ending up with a warning about eating too much watermelon, especially before bedtime. I grew up, along with all my cousins, and nearly forgot the story, until many years ago at a family reunion in Kansas, I was reminiscing with my cousin Hugh.

"And Hugh," I laughed, "Remember Grandpa Fox's famous watermelon dream?"

"What dream?" Hugh asked, puzzled. "I don't remember that one."

"Surely you remember," I pressed. "Remember sitting around outdoors in the evening, slurping up all that wonderful melon and listening to Grandpa Fox tell his story of that fabulous adventure?"

"No," Hugh insisted. "I don't remember any such story."

So, I asked cousin after cousin, doubting Hugh's memory, and not my own, and found no one else — not even my older brother Dick — who recalled Grandpa Fox's famous watermelon dream.

For a long time, many years in fact, I felt smug about my ability to remember such an extraordinary story, while everyone else seemed to be stricken by a strange amnesia. Finally, I began to consider the possibility that I myself had the faulty memory, that the events described never really happened at all, or happened in some other context. I began to ponder the whole phenomenon of memory, how it evolves out of one's mind, how a germ of 'objective' truth may be wrought over the years into layers of story, how the story itself becomes the 'truth.' It occurs to me as I write this, many decades hence, that perhaps Grandpa Fox's famous watermelon dream, cherished over the years — was my own.

* * *

Because of my Grandpa Fox's success as a provider, my grandmother was able to hire girls to help with housekeeping and childrearing—as well as a dressmaker, a Mrs. Powers, who sewed the girls' dresses while her 'weird' (Aunt Eva's word) son spied on them. As was the fashion at the time, the three younger girls were dressed alike, most likely attracting the admiration and possibly envy of many Longford townspeople, who might not be able to afford such niceties. This extra help enabled Cora to teach piano to her own children, as well as many others in the area. She could read music as well as play by ear, often listening intently to a tune on the radio.

"I think I can play that," she would say, making her way to the piano. After humming a little and flirting with a few chords, her curved nails clicking on the keys, she would reconstruct the radio tune, entertaining and amazing us all. Throughout my life, I have tried in vain to follow in my grandmother's musical footsteps, never becoming the musician she was and never being able to play, as she could, by ear.

My father and his sisters learned to play other instruments, so at one time they comprised a little family band, playing together at least once a week, especially on Sunday evenings. Don played the sax, Ruth the alto sax, with Eva on soprano sax. Mary played the trombone, and Genevieve (according to Ruth) played "bad violin." In spite of the dubious mentoring of an often-drunk saxophone teacher, with my grandmother's help, they struggled through old favorites, such as *Red Sails in the Sunset* and *The Band Played On*. Sometimes, to liven things up, Eva would sing and tap dance to *Has Anybody Seen My Gal?*

Many years later, after my parents got together and had my older brother and me, Sundays were associated with music, then in the form of popular big band records of the day. Before my family became involved in the Episcopal Church, rushing breakfast to arrive in time for my father and me to robe up for the choir, we sinfully lounged around on Sunday mornings, my dad making waffles, while we all seemed to glide around on the smooth graphite tones of Tommy Dorsey, Artie Shaw and the "incomparable," as radio DJs used to say, Benny Goodman.

How my family became involved in and dedicated to, the Episcopal Church is a story in itself. My own part in this story comes from a time long before the life changing event. I seemed to have developed, at an early age, a yearning for the 'holy.' Whenever Bible classes were offered to kids whose parents approved, I eagerly lined up with several of my grade school classmates to walk the couple of blocks to a nearby church and listen attentively to stories about Jesus.

They seemed a bit like the wonderful fairy tales I grew up with, full of miracles, with Jesus being the hero. Yet, I didn't really "receive the spirit," as they say, and took to arranging little altars in my bedroom, complete with Bible, vase of flowers picked from my mother's flowerbeds, and some kind of cross—all prettily displayed on a clean linen cloth of some sort. I also began praying, kneeling by my bed each night to recite the *Now I Lay Me* prayer, ending with all the 'blesses'—mother, father, etc., etc. Still, I was left with an unsettling yearning for—something.

When I was around 10 years old, that 'something' began to evolve after my family—en masse—eagerly accepted the invitation to attend St. John's Episcopal Church in downtown Wichita, after an unusual sort of conversion. A few months before, my father, scanning the newspaper while nursing a bad cold, came upon an ad, asking for an 'exchange'—a twelve unit furnished motel with office/home in Tempe, Arizona—for a furnished home 'somewhere' away from the Southwest.

Although this should have raised all kinds of red flags, the ad instead caught my parents' imagination. My father pictured himself the casual owner of an attractive motel, being filled each night by travelers on vacation. And my mother envisioned the end of her dreadful pleurisy and allergies. Never mind that both were heavy smokers, who never made the connection between health issues and their smoking (cigarettes for my mother, pipes and cigars for my father). Couple this with a restlessness they both felt, uncertainty over the prospect of my father's new job involving a lot of travel—which my mother, especially, disliked — and the fantasy of a new life in a warmer climate with lots of sunshine.

Alas, this fairy tale was doomed to collapse. After realizing that their newly acquired motel — named the 'Hi-Ohio' to attract visitors from Ohio, the previous owners' home state — was set on a major highway with dozens of competing motels surrounding them, many with enticing swimming pools, they grew discouraged, then panicky. My father, who had joined us after finishing up his work at Derby Oil Company, even tried to attract prospective customers by driving in and out of our circular driveway, to make it seem how popular we were. After a few days of sizing up the situation, he high-tailed it back to Wichita and managed to plead for his old job (he always was a good salesman), leaving my mother, two brothers and my paternal grandparents, who were 'vacationing' with us, to wait out the hoped-for sale of our pathetic little motel.

My mother began to further damage her health by taking on all the chores of running a motel: cleaning the units, laundering all the linens, tending to often cranky visitors — at the same time trying to hold the family together.

One miserable afternoon, while on her knees scrubbing the floor of one of the units, she thought to herself, "While I'm on my knees, I may as well pray." And pray she did, desperately, for a buyer to save us all from what had become a terrible mistake.

According to her, it was a matter of days—if not the next day—when a buyer appeared, an offer was accepted, and we all moved back to Kansas, and our lives as churchgoing believers began.

So, I stopped building altars in my bedroom and immersed myself, at age 8 or so, into the seductive aesthetics of the Episcopal Church. I have been inside and outside the church door my entire adult life, but at the beginning—and for the adolescent/young adult stage of my life—I was in love: with the liturgy, the music, the stained glass, the dark carved woodwork and red carpets covering the kneeling pads that cleverly lowered from the backs of pews for prayers. Hymns were for standing; lessons and sermons for sitting.

As for belief, I followed my parents and older brother Dick to the Baptismal font, then soon after, to attend the stern instruction of Father James Hoffman, our rector, in order to receive Confirmation. I believed, though, because I was in love. And like all lovers, I trusted the beloved. God seeped into my body and made a soul, which he has fed—in one way or another—my entire life. Though now, for me God is larger than the Episcopal Church, larger than any church or belief or creed. God is the summation of the universe, and like the Tao, cannot be named.

III

While my father was enjoying his pampered, somewhat privileged, upbringing, my mother was finally relieved of her farm chores when the family moved to Kansas City during my grandfather's tenure in the State, and then the National, Farmer's Union, which he served for several years as president. My grandmother, Lizzie, had refused to follow her husband to the big bad city and continued to run the farm with the children until none of them could stand it any longer, and they all moved to Kansas City. Lizzie discovered, to her surprise, that she loved shopping the many vegetable stands near the Plaza, and she quickly made friends with her neighbors, with whom she was often in competition as to who could get her laundry out first on Monday mornings.

Unfortunately, my mother's entry into junior high school was accompanied by much humiliation. Grandma Lizzie did not know anything about the fashion world and did not think it demeaning for her elder daughter to go to school wearing dresses made from flour sacks. Rather than let this get her down, my mother resolved to sew her own clothes and even before she knew about patterns would lie on top of selected material, called 'yard goods' at that time, and draw in chalk around her form. I imagine the results were not much better than the shapeless flour sack dresses, but her dressmaking skills improved over time, until later in life she was able to sew virtually anything, including upholstery, lined drapes, my younger brother's prom tuxedo and my own college wardrobe featuring sophisticated Vogue designs and lovely expensive fabrics.

By the time she was in high school, my mother had resolved to overcome her country second-generation Czech inferiority complex and her own body's adolescent awkwardness. She began to excel in journalism, becoming the editor of the Wyandotte High School newspaper. Later, bored with the usual small talk of such publications, she began to emulate the comic strip idol Brenda Starr by scooping stories about celebrities who frequently entertained in Kansas City. These she offered to the Kansas City Star. She sometimes hid in dressing room closets to get interviews and once was dragged home by her older brother Al from a speakeasy where she was trying to get her story. One time, Eddie Cantor came to town, and apparently mistaking my mother for someone he knew, grabbed and kissed her passionately before he realized his 'mistake.' This story was validated, when a recent visit with my brother Dick and family produced a signed photograph of Eddie Cantor, addressed to 'Fern.' Another time, my mother managed to interview Walt Disney, who also worked for the Star, and reported his eccentric fascination with the caged mice he kept and drew — in the process, of course, creating his world-famous *Mickey Mouse.*

My mother's journalistic success was given the credit she craved in the school yearbook, which featured a glamorous full-page portrait of her, showing her medium-long hair parted on the side and waved, Lana Turner style, down one side of her face. Being tall, she also enjoyed and excelled in girls basketball. But my grandfather wanted her to acquire the social graces befitting a young city girl, so she was enrolled in what were then called charm classes, which, unbeknownst to my mother, were to terminate in a graduation, or coming out, ceremony given for the parents and friends of the now 'finished' young ladies.

Understandably, my mother became bored with these classes and escaped to the YWCA to swim, not realizing she would ultimately be humiliated by a public exposure of her choosing fun over Emily Post. While the other young ladies sat demurely waiting for their turn to be introduced, my mother squirmed in her chair and awkwardly tried to mimic their paces when her turn came. Another embarrassment occurred at a violin recital in which my mother, so nervous over the performance of a duet with her teacher, finished her part and placed her violin in its case before her teacher had even finished playing. Clearly, she was not destined for the stage.

These humiliations later inspired multiple lessons for me in modeling, baton twirling, ballet and piano—this last pursuit being the only one that actually stuck. I later wondered why these lessons were foisted upon me, when my mother herself was conflicted about their value.

After high school graduation, Fern expected to study at Kansas State College. But my strict grandfather, adhering to practicality and old-world ways, refused, insisting that the older boys, Al and Steve, had to finish first. Angry, but not discouraged, she managed to win a partial scholarship at Drake University in Des Moines, Iowa, and began her college career there, far away from home. She often told us stories of her hardships there, babysitting for faculty and cleaning sorority houses to supplement her scholarship.

It was during this time that she caught the attention of Dr. Daniel Morehouse, an astronomy professor for whom the Morehouse Comet is named, who paid my mother to transcribe his learned articles into laymen's language for publication in non-professional journals.

"He never realized how hard a task this was," she told us. "He thought I just whipped them up in a few hours, when I actually would stay up nights working on those projects!"

She also became dazed and confused, looking through telescopes at the vast night sky, trying to understand his ideas. So, she finally gave up working for him, especially when he began to pressure her to accompany him to China to continue transcribing his research. China! So far away from Kansas, almost as far as the stars, it must have seemed to her.

At last, my grandfather, realizing how serious my mother was about her schooling, consented to her enrollment at Kansas State College. She returned home, continued her journalism studies at Kedzie Hall, joined the Alpha Zi Delta sorority and began at long last to have a social life.

IV

While my mother was floundering through charm school and violin lessons in Kansas City, at last finding her niche in journalism, my father was enjoying his adolescence at Longford High School (graduating class of less than 50). Being both bright and handsome, he had no trouble with schoolwork — and no problem attracting a flock of adoring girlfriends. Tall, with wavy, honey-colored hair and a slender elegant nose, he also possessed those clear blue eyes that found their genetic paths into so many of my Fox relatives.

My father loved to tell us a couple of anecdotes, now legendary, about his early school days. He often repeated to us how he had to walk *two miles* to school and back every day, even during famous Kansas blizzards that piled up drifts as tall as he was and blinded farmers, who groped their way to barns in order to feed hungry livestock. Many years later, when he showed us around Longford and pointed out the houses where the family had lived, we gleefully exposed his exaggeration: "But Daddy, none of your houses was more than a few blocks away from either of the schools!"

Another story involved a transgression of one of the pupils attending the one-room elementary school in Longford. Neither the guilty child, nor any of his classmates, would confess the truth. So, the teacher, a strapping young man not about to be cowed by a roomful of country brats, lined up all of them facing the wall to endure their punishment: a resounding whack of the wooden paddle on their tender behinds. One by one, the teacher stood behind each pupil— *whack! whack! whack!* while the others winced and closed their eyes, terrified, awaiting their turn.

It wasn't until after school when the children all compared notes (how hard did he hit you?) that they realized the teacher had simply whacked the paddle against something he had held in his other hand—and that none of them had been paddled at all! The cleverness, not to mention kindness, of the teacher had won him the respect and obedience of his pupils, and there was no more deception after that.

When my father finished high school, he automatically matriculated into Kansas State, where he became a freshman enrolled in chemical engineering. As a matter of fact, nearly all college-bound relatives of my parents' generation on both sides of the family attended Kansas State, at that time (the early 30s), mostly an agricultural college. He took easily to campus life, joining Kappa Sigma fraternity in the heyday of such organizations, dressing as a young man about campus and driving his girlfriends around in the Ford given him by my grandfather.

So how did they meet—my ambitious and industrious mother and my handsome, charming father? Since he was a year older than she, and because she had spent a year at Drake University, they did not cross paths until one night in her sophomore year, when they both attended a college dance with their dates. Actually, my father was 'unofficially' engaged at the time. My future parents were instantly attracted to each other, danced together—and before the evening wound down, they were passionately in love, shamelessly abandoning their dates and driving off together. According to my dad's sisters, the pair were inseparable, dating furiously, attending all the sorority and fraternity parties together, while trying to study and keep up their grades.

A few years ago, when my father lay in a hospital bed awaiting his death from cancer (and after my mother had died), he confessed to a love tryst in the office of K-State's president. Apparently, my mother had permission to research some files for an article, and my dad insisted they eat their bag lunches together in the president's office while he was away at lunch. They locked the door, and, as my dad sheepishly recalled, but not without relish, "Well, one thing led to another…"

V

The couple's courtship did not go unnoticed by their families, and before long, all of them had met. My dad's sisters tell of an incident which cemented their admiration for their future sister-in-law. The details are unclear, but they agree that my mother saved the day for them at a picnic at Tonganoxie Lake, near Kansas City, where the sisters had decided to (float, swim, boat?) out to a moored platform on the lake. They panicked when they decided they were unable to make it back to shore. My mother somehow swam out to rescue them, one by one, demonstrating her skill as a swimmer. I find this story puzzling, since later in their lives, when my parents designed and built a wonderful house on Lake Hamilton, near Hot Springs, Arkansas, my mother rarely went into the water—and I never ever saw her actually swim. When quizzed about this, she said that she didn't like the fish "nibbling on (her) moles."

On the 19th of September, 1933, my passionate parents decided—the Depression be damned—that they would run off to a neighboring county to be married secretly by a Justice of the Peace. Though exciting enough at the time, the secret elopement robbed my mother of a 'real wedding' with frocked minister, cake, flowers, etc., so that she always felt cheated of this experience. Later, when their grown children gave them a catered 50th anniversary party — complete with layered cake and marzipan decorations — she always referred to this celebration as 'the wedding.'

Why my parents decided to keep their marriage a secret is unclear; perhaps it had something to do with their housing arrangements at the fraternity and sorority houses where they were living. They may have already paid for their lodging and could not afford to give up the remaining time. At any rate, when my mother became pregnant with my older brother after only five months, they were forced out of the closet — and out of their housing. They took up various residences, variously pathetic, as they awaited his birth. At one time, they lived in a railroad car, until they moved up in the world to a real apartment with a real kitchen area and bathroom. Never mind that it had only one room and that my mother had to hang my brother's diapers indoors to dry. He was born in November, and Kansas winters did not permit much drying out of doors.

Of the birth itself, my mother told us, with no small degree of bitterness, that she was attended by a 'horse doctor,' who delayed coming to the apartment until "you can see the top of the baby's head." My mother, completely naive about childbirth—thanks to my old-country grandmother who was probably embarrassed to discuss such things with her daughter—did not expect the birth to be so painful. During the increasingly rapid contractions, she even tried to make the pain go away by standing on her head in the corner.

Miraculously, my brother was born in Augusta, Kansas, on November 21, 1934, close to Thanksgiving Day. I have always been thankful that both he and my mother survived the birth. Since she had had no prenatal care, she had eaten whatever and as much as she pleased, not realizing that much of the extra nourishment would produce a ten-pound baby boy, whom they named Donald—after my father—and Richard (one of those names parents picked out of a book, perhaps to avoid choosing another family name). My father had gotten a job at a refinery near Wichita and was able to just barely support his little family. My mother, bending to the conventional (and unfortunate) wisdom of the times, gave up her college study—and a budding career in journalism—to be a full-time wife and mother. Judging from an endearing letter she wrote to 'Little Dickie,' her darling son, she had not yet become disillusioned about her role as wife and mother and showered loving adoration on her husband and son.

My father, it seems, viewed fatherhood as a responsibility, while the child himself was seen as another plaything who was sometimes amusing—and at other times demanding to be amused. One of Dick's first Christmases, my mother took off for the afternoon to shop. Trying to comfort his bawling son, my father took him on his lap to look at "all the pretty glass balls" on the tree. My brother became bored with this low-key activity and began again to cry, forcing my father to come up with something more amusing.

In desperation, he dug out an air pistol, and taking careful aim, at the same time holding Dick on his lap, began—one by one—to pop the brightly colored balls on the tree. At last, this not only proved vastly more amusing to my brother, who gurgled with delight, but to my father, who (by his own account) laughed uproariously after every direct hit. My mother, needless to say, was the only one in the family not amused to find her Christmas tree so violated—and colored glass all over the floor.

Fortunately, my brother survived the various entertainments my father provided for him, but he very nearly did not survive an accident that befell him as a toddler. For the first several years of his life, he had enjoyed the chance distinction of being the first grandchild on both sides of the family, and as such soaked up the attention and adoration of grandparents, as well as numerous aunts and uncles who had not started their families—some had not even married yet—and who appropriately fussed over 'Little Dickie.' A black-and-white photo shows him sitting contentedly in the sun, a pair of oversized sunglasses set askew on his pudgy, dimpled face.

The incident which caused so much distress in the family—and which nearly cost him his life—began innocently enough. In the family's little second story apartment, my brother, apparently trying to avoid a bath, ran away from my mother and crawled onto a window sill by way of a couch, which had been pushed up to the wall under the window. It was summer, and the window was open. The screen, which was fastened by a simple hook, gave way to the weight of my brother, who had pressed against it. My mother, who told of the incident many times over the years, claimed that she ran down the stairs so fast she was outside in the front yard before my brother, having luckily landed first on an awning over a ground floor window, hit the ground.

He lived, but the fractures in his left leg were so severe he was put into two separate leg and body casts to accommodate his growth. Over the course of many months, he was forced to lie still, his leg held back and curved like a scorpion's tail, while my mother and other family members read books to him and tried to keep him quiet. Needless to say, the entire episode was traumatic, both for mother and child. After the casts were cut away, the doctor announced to my horrified parents that, while the fractures had healed, my brother's left leg would most likely grow no more—and that he would suffer his life as a cripple, carrying around one three-year-old leg, useless and pitiful.

This prognosis my mother refused to accept, and she resolved that Dick would not only have a useful limb, but that it would grow normally as well. Her treatment, carried out religiously over many months, was to massage my brother's leg, day after day, for many hours, and pull on the tendons which had shrunk and prevented his left heel from reaching the ground when he walked. Of course, these treatments were quite painful, drawing tears to the eyes of both mother and son.

There are photos of my brother, wearing a special shoe with an elevated heel that was gradually reduced over the course of years—even after I entered the family, when he was nearly six years old. After the War, I remember going to a special orthopedic shoe store in Wichita, where Dick was fitted for new shoes. I enjoyed placing my stockinged feet under a scope, which magically revealed their startling skeletons, looking nothing like the appendages I put into shoes each day.

My brother healed. His bones knitted. His tendons relaxed and allowed normal growth. The only reminder of this interlude in his life—besides the terror of the accident itself and the mental and physical pain he suffered — is his left foot, which is a whole size smaller than his right.

For a long time after this accident, and its long months of healing, my brother suffered the mental anguish of stuttering, which fortunately, he was able to overcome with therapy.

VI

By the time I entered this world, and became a part of the family I would grow to love, all my aunts and uncles on both sides had married: Aunt Marie to William Larson; Uncle Steve to Mary Emily Baum; Uncle Al to Verla Waggoner (on my mother's side). And Aunt Genevieve to 'Bud' Emrich; Aunt Ruth to Cleason ('C.K.') Minter; Aunt Mary to Lawrence Cooney; Aunt Eva to George Kathary (on my father's side). I had also been preceded by Verla Jean, a cousin a bit younger than my brother, daughter of Uncle Al and Aunt Verla, and by three boy cousins born a couple of months before me: Larry Don (to Aunt Mary and Uncle Lawrence), Hugh (to Aunt Genevieve and Uncle Bud) and John (to Uncle Steve and Aunt Mary Emily—always called 'Aunt Bing' because Uncle Steve thought she looked Chinese when she braided her hair at bedtime, and thus nicknamed her Bing-Baum). I myself always thought that 'Aunt Mary Em' would have been a more dignified nickname, and more befitting her personality.

I was born at 6:13 am on August 13, 1940, at Wesley Hospital in Wichita, Kansas. I weighed in at 6 pounds 13 ounces, a good deal lighter than my older brother. All these 13s seemed especially fortuitous, since my maternal grandfather, John Vesecky, had been born on May 13, 1879. He must have especially appreciated this connection, since he sent a telegram to my mother in her hospital room (she had demanded an easier labor this time!):

Congratulations upon the birth of a granddaughter letter on the way. Lots of love.

– Dad John

I was promptly named Mary Elizabeth Fox: Elizabeth for my maternal grandmother (always called "Lizzie") and Mary for my maternal great-aunt and, of course, my Aunt Mary. This choice must have disappointed my brother Dick, who had favored the name Judy Franklin for me. Since my paternal grandfather's name is Franklin, I can understand that. I have no idea where the Judy came from. I actually never felt comfortable with the name Mary, though I was called Mary Elizabeth (or simply M.E.) throughout my early years, and I later dropped the Mary in favor of Liz, the name I use now. If I had had a say in my naming, I would have called myself Augusta, after my maternal great-grandmother, especially since I was born in August, which by the way, was not a month I would have chosen either, it being extremely hot and dry in Kansas at that time. My mother had rejected Augusta, because she feared it would be shortened to Gussie or Gus, which she did not like at all.*

My mother also received a bouquet of flowers from Derby Oil Company, where my father was employed (and would continue to be until 1958, the year of my high school graduation). By this time, he had begun taking and developing his own photographs, so my nude baby pictures were added to my brother's (not nude) photos in the family album. My father also began collecting prizes for some of these. I guess photography was a welcome respite from his work at the refinery, and a chance to use his chemistry skills in a more creative way. In my early years, I was embarrassed by all these naked baby pictures. Later, I was amused by my homeliness: close-set eyes, little hair to speak of (though I would grow volumes of the blond stuff throughout my life) and drooling grin. I was always skinny as a child, but in these pictures, I am quite plump.

A couple of years or so later, another tier of cousins followed me, like decorations on a wedding cake: Fen (to Uncle Steve and Aunt Bing); Judy (my brother

---

* As of this writing, I have legally changed my name to Augusta Elizabeth Fox Vesecky.

finally prevailed!) to Aunt Eva and Uncle George; Kathy, or Kathleen, (to Aunt Ruth and Uncle Cleason); Diane (to Aunt Mary and Uncle Lawrence); Connie to Uncle Al and his second wife Betty, and Christy (to Aunt Marie and Uncle Bill). At the age of two, Christy died quite suddenly from meningitis, breaking the hearts of my Uncle Bill and Aunt Marie, who was already pregnant with little Stevie. Later, when Stevie was still an infant, he was saved from a similar fate by my mother, who administered a rather mystical regimen of timed teaspoonfuls of sugared water, somehow bringing him around. Christy's sudden death, and my Aunt's terrible grief, shocked and frightened me. It was my first experience of death, and since it occurred during wartime when I was about four, it gave new meaning to the dying of soldiers overseas.

I always liked my cousins and enjoyed sending letters written on fancy stationary with matching envelops, and getting similar ones in return: "How are you? I am fine. When are you coming to visit?" etc. I especially looked forward to family get-togethers that would allow much romping about and kid fun. I must say I was a bit wary of Hugh and Fen, who teased me by dogging my steps and taking every opportunity to pinch me or pull one of my thick braids (my hair finally did come in). Larry Don was funny and made me laugh, imitating the cowboy heroes we watched at

Saturday movie matinées, especially *The Lone Ranger* and *Roy Rogers*, always with Dale Evans at his side.

My cousin John I adored from the first. I was about three or four when Uncle Steve and Aunt Bing came up from Dallas to visit us. This was during the war, and my mother and brother and I were living with Grandpa John and Grandma Lizzie in Kansas City. We were seated at the dining table for lunch.

John, who was dressed in white short pants with suspenders and white short-sleeved shirt (along with white socks and sandals), kept leaving the table every bite he took, in order to chew it privately, facing the wall. I thought this behavior wonderfully strange, and I always held my brown-haired, brown-eyed cousin in high regard because of this.

Though I don't remember anything of my first eighteen months of life, I have the impression that this was a good time for my family. My father was progressing in his career, my mother appeared to be happy in her role as wife and mother, and my brother Dick, recovered from his injury at last, began to play as a normal boy, filling his role as the apple of my eye. This idyllic state was not to last. Europe was already at war, and Pearl Harbor was about to change all our lives.

VII
The Other War

Shadow Soldiers

It was a long trip. My brother and I lay on top of quilts covering luggage and other personal effects, while my mother sat in front with her war-wife friend Gerry, who drove so badly that my mother took the wheel and learned to drive on the spot. We stared at the open endless landscape and felt the absence of my father, now on his way to Honolulu and the war. Both he and my uncle George were called into the service from the ROTC reserves: my father as a Second Lieutenant to the Air Force, and Uncle George to the Army, in which he served as a First Lieutenant in the C.I.C. (Counter Intelligence Core) in Okinawa and the Philippines. Another uncle, Al, joined the Navy and was stationed in the Arctic somewhere, and then in Guatemala. At some point during the war, he sent home a Navy parka with wolf fur trim that has been worn by several members of the family over the years, as well as colorful Guatemalan clothes and leather huarache sandals. When I first wore them at dinner, my family kept asking, "What is that squeaking noise?" As we listened, the noise stopped, but resumed once conversation began. In time, it became amusingly clear that the squeaking was the result of my moving my feet in the new sandals, under the table.

We had said goodbye to my father in San Francisco, where, because I was fearlessly active, I had to be harnessed when taken out on the streets of the strange city, and where I had embarrassed my parents by peeing on the lush carpets at the 'Top of the Mark.' I was nineteen months old, and these stories were told to me later. I knew nothing then of the dangers my father might encounter, nor did I feel my mother's anxiety. War was a word I had not learned, and my infant thoughts had not yet become memory.

I began to remember things in Kansas City, where we lived with my maternal grandparents on Mercier Street, not far from downtown and the Plaza. My grandfather Vesecky was working for the Farmer's Union Jobbing Association, having previously served as its national president for several terms. During this time, he was in communication with Secretary of Agriculture Henry A. Wallace, and with FDR himself. He had managed years before to coax my grandmother off their farm in Timken, so she could take her place beside him, and ultimately, take charge of an anxious daughter and two 'fatherless' grandchildren, along with numerous other relatives who lived with them from time to time during the war.

Gradually, we became a family, the difference being that my grandparents became our parents, and my mother faded into the background at this time, overwhelmed by what I assume now to be fear and her sense of displacement. I don't remember being close to her during those years. I'm sure she took care of me, and yet it was the stern discipline of Grandpa John I feared and respected; and it was the gruff, yet tender, protection of Grandma Lizzie I sought and enjoyed — to the extent that she took my side in every early childhood conflict I encountered, with the result that I became quite spoiled and headstrong. Both of my grandparents brought their Czech endurance to this new challenge, having grown up in the harsh environment of western Kansas, living first in dugouts, and tilling the rocky, unforgiving soil.

Neither of my Vesecky grandparents were large or overbearing in appearance, being rather of average height and weight. But both had a compactness about them and an economy of movement that projected strength. Their arms and hands were farmers' arms and hands — capable, practiced in the land. Grandma's speech, more than Grandpa's, contained remnants of Czech accents and rhythms and was full of folk wisdom which was planted in me to take root, grow and blossom in the future.

I was with Grandma practically all day. She fixed my breakfasts of hard-boiled eggs mashed up with butter, and glasses of milk with globs of cream floating on top. I loved the butter, and I would often steal the rationed gold off the table. But the floating cream in my milk didn't seem right somehow, and I would spoon it off the top. I never got punished for this finicky behavior, since Grandma would later lick the cream from my spoon, as she licked chicken fat from our noodle soup bowls at lunch. I think Grandma was saving for the war in this way, never eating much on her own plate, but making up for it by eating whatever anyone else left.

After breakfast, we would wash clothes, dust-mop the floors with the fragrant cedar-oiled mop, or do the marketing, depending on what day it was. I liked the marketing best, even though I had to be dragged along at Grandma's furious pace, both of us clutching oversized pocketbooks and wearing high-top shoes— hers black, mine white. The shopping took us past towering apartment houses that fascinated me because of their size, and because of the swing sets and teeter-totters in the small play yards below. I wanted to swing every time we passed these apartments, but Grandma said no, they belonged to the children who lived there, the children I never ever saw swinging on them.

We also passed through the Plaza with its exciting fountains and big stores with windows full of artificial ladies wearing suits and hats and gloves. But it was the vegetables my grandma was after. She had left her big farm garden near Timken, and she sought its replacement on the city streets lined by shops with crates full of tomatoes, turnips, potatoes, onions, carrots and beets. And she wanted them perfect, driving the shopkeepers crazy, pinching and weighing them, until I tired and begged to be taken home.

(Perhaps it was these shopping trips that emboldened me to begin my early morning wanderings, told to me years later. An early riser, I somehow managed to open the front door and stroll the empty sidewalks, singing nursery rhymes to myself. Once a neighbor phoned our house, asking, "Is this your little girl wandering alone through the neighborhood?" I often wonder now whether I may have been sleepwalking, since in later years, I sometimes woke up lying on the kitchen floor in front of the stove — or other places — in our Wichita house).

Lunch was Grandma's chicken noodle soup with mashed potatoes, and sometimes we had custard sprinkled with nutmeg that was served in small deep cups, all of different colors. We ate, my brother and I, in a carved wooden booth in the kitchen near a window where the sun streamed in and made a delicious drowsy blend of the yellow soup and yellow custard.

Then Grandma and I took a nap. She didn't trust me, I guess, and always lay down beside me, pretending to be asleep while I worried about the cobwebs in the corners above my bed. Grandma Lizzie cleaned every day, but there were always cobwebs. Formed by dust blowing from heat registers in the floor, they appeared as gauzy threats hovering over us. They bothered me, as did the intense voices from the radio we listened to every night, and I often wouldn't sleep until Grandma had swept all the cobwebs away.

The radio broadcasts focused the uneasiness I felt much of the time, despite my grandma's protection. After supper, the rounded brown wooden box in the living room was turned on, and voices sputtered out of it, voices that told us of battles and whether or not the 'Japs' had invaded Pearl Harbor again. And although I did not understand the fuzzy words, I knew my father was there somewhere in the radio voice, as he was in the vast blue of the Pacific Ocean I was shown on the globe of the world, as he was also in the framed photo of a man I kissed through the glass every night before going to bed—a handsome man in a uniform with bars and stripes.

It was Gabriel Heater we listened to most, and when he announced, "It's good news tonight," I could play and stay up late. If he said, "It's bad news tonight," I was whisked off to bed and spent the evening with my brother Dick and our cousin Verla

Jean, trying to sneak back into the living room. Grandma had managed to get Verla Jean to come to Kansas from California, because the 'Japs' might any minute decide to bomb California, where she had been living with her mother, Aunt Verla—and then what would happen to cousin V.J.? Such was the argument Grandma Lizzie insisted upon as she lay on the couch, refusing to eat, cook or speak—until Grandpa relented and paid the train fare for V.J. to join us.

So, the three of us plastered ourselves against our shadows on the hall wall and tried to edge toward the living room. It became a game played to the rhythm of a tense voice from a wooden box, and we became soldiers with bayonets and helmets in a jungle of shadows.

* * *

Laundry

Getting clothes and linens clean was a ritual, a duty and a devotion. The process—from dropping soiled dresses down the chute in the upstairs bathroom, to pulling clean ones over my head in the morning, intrigued me; and Grandma's fierce devotion to the weekly task was shared by me, her apprentice.

She used her own homemade soap. The store-bought soap in cardboard boxes was suspicious to her, and she spent hours in the dark and musty cellar with the washing machine and rinse tubs—mixing, boiling, straining and pouring liquid lye soap in trays to harden. Afterward, she cut the crude, oily-soft bars to be shaved into the washer or rubbed with stubbornly spotted clothes against a washboard that I ran my fingers up and down while watching. My fascination with laundry was rewarded with a birthday gift of a miniature washer and ringer rinse tub that really worked. Washing my doll clothes and hanging them in the sun with tiny wooden pins was one of my greatest pleasures.

Grandma would sort and pile the soiled clothes and linens, feed them into the churning washer, then rinse and run them through the hand turned wringer. Finally, the clean, wet clothes were heaped into a basket to be hung outdoors in the sun. It was a contest to see which of the neighborhood women got her washing out first, and Grandma was almost always first. She rewarded herself with a cup of coffee, which she smugly sipped on the front porch, while the other women were still laboring with their laundry.

I sat still, watching Grandma's strong forearms above the steaming wash tubs, smelling the clean hot smell of lye and bleach, watching the dirt disappear in streams of dark warm water circling into a drain in the cement cellar floor. I sensed somehow that this passion, this effort and energy, was another part of Grandma's war effort, as if her spotless laundry were a testimony to goodness and purity, and an antidote to the horrors which spilled into our lives through the radio broadcasts, the newspapers with headlines big as grave stones and letters from the soldiers who never said how bad it really was.

* * *

Ragman

Once in a while, usually in the afternoon just before I was to take my nap, Grandma would mysteriously draw the shades, hurry me away from the windows, holding a forefinger in front of her tightly closed lips. For a long time, I never knew the cause of this strange behavior, and sat wondering if the war had started in our city, and if Hitler's troops were marching down our streets, their stiff legs thrown out in front of them.

Finally, one day I caught a glimpse of a figure on the sidewalk, just before Grandma closed the shade. It was a man, dressed in dark ragged clothing, holding a cloth bag over his shoulder. He walked in a sort of slow shuffle, with his head bowed, as though he were ashamed of what he was doing.

"It's the ragman," Grandma finally told me. "He's coming to beg for our old clothes."

Though he frightened me, Grandma's behavior frightened me more. Why, if he were poor and only wanted our old clothes, didn't we open the door to him, instead of shutting him out in such a shameful way? Why, if we could beg for newspapers to help end the war, couldn't we also give to this poor, dark-looking man? It was shameful, I thought—as shameful as the shuffle of the man with his drooping head.

What I did not understand then was my grandmother's proud, old-world ways. She didn't open the door because she, too, was ashamed, and would rather have the ragman think we were not at home, than to tell him we had no clothes to give.

* * *

Hitler's Picture

In my brother's room was a poster-sized picture of Adolf Hitler. It was an ugly picture, made worse by holes that looked like pock marks all over his face. The holes were concentrated in the center of his face, around the nose, mouth and eyes, and were caused by darts thrown at the picture for sport by my brother and cousin V.J., and sometimes even by me.

It was a delicious sport, yet cruel; for while we knew our actions were guiltless and that Hitler was a bad man, we also knew somehow that the hatred was in itself also bad. That were the picture of anyone else, our actions would have been punished, rather than tolerated and even encouraged. So, we played, aiming the darts at the most vital parts, cheering each other on, applauding the hits and near hits, as though we were participating in a much larger, more desperate battle.

And the picture of Hitler worsened day by day, month by month, until the eyes themselves were only dark holes, the mouth a gaping wound, the paper flesh torn and shredded. And for me, the pleasure had gone out of torturing the picture of this evil man. I wished the paper flesh to be restored, the picture to be rolled up and thrown away. I wanted the closet door on which the picture was tacked to be bare, and all the holes to be filled and smoothed so that the wood shone with its own grain, and was itself once again.

* * *

Christy

When she arrived, I was no longer the little one. Grandma's lap held another little girl, two years younger than I, and different. While I had blond curls and green eyes, she had dark brown wispy hair, cheeks full and red as sand plums and large round brown eyes. She sat on Grandma's lap on the front porch on summer evenings and made *oooh* sounds with the wind. Grandma would say, "Oooh…oooh," and Christy would answer her, and the wind would answer them both.

I wasn't a part of this game, but I stood and watched them both, and felt a feeling I would only later attach a word to. It was the first time I had felt this feeling, and it was not pleasant. But this was Aunt Marie and Uncle Bill's little girl — and my cousin, who I realized might someday grow bigger and be a playmate. Though Grandma might continue to hold and play with her, I would no longer be alone, and favored, in my smallness.

But Christy got sick one day. She was wrapped in a blanket and carried away, and she didn't come back. All of a sudden, she was just gone. No more pretty brown-eyed little girl in white dresses talking to the wind. Just Aunt Marie, throwing herself across a bed and sobbing, and me, looking at the bottoms of her shoes, not knowing how to make her stop crying, not knowing the name of this feeling inside.

* * *

Nightmares

I could not, would not, be stilled. I screamed and cried hysterically, inconsolably, even though I was aware of the faces and hands of those trying to calm me: my mother, her red hair wild from her own troubled sleep, entreating me, smiling through her own fears; Grandma Lizzie, promising pennies, nickels even, if I would just stop crying; my cousin Verla Jean, promising her favorite dolls for me to play with in some unimaginable future called 'the next day' — if I would only stop; my grandfather, even, his husky voice full of concern, pleading reason.

These faces, these hands, could only blur the surface of those dreams from which I could not awake, though my eyes were open and I sat upright. They seemed instead extensions of the dreams themselves, horrid in their distorted familiarity, images waving before me, coming in and out of focus, at first small, then larger — so close to my face, they only increased my terror, my cries.

I do not remember those dreams, whether they were inhabited by monsters worse even than Hitler, making hellish sounds like the war brought over the radio—warplanes in screeching dives, crackling explosions. I only remember not being able to awake from the horrors, not being able to break through the membrane of dream life into 'real' life, where I could clasp the cold coins, play with Verla Jean's dolls.

* * *

Flamingo Pink: Blue Hills

During the last two years or so of the war, in the midst of radio broadcasts, newspaper headlines and rationing, I began to grow aware of something other than my fears, and the chaos that surrounded them. It began with the pictures on the backs of playing cards left for my amusement. I studied the strange birds with long, skinny legs and beaks that made a corner. They were flamingos, I learned, and I took in their color the way I took in sunlight. I knew pink. And there was blue, too—blue in the hills I gazed at, sitting on the sidewalk on Mercier Street, watching the clouds move and change as the sun went down. Pink, blue. Different pink, different blue.

Some older girls lived in the neighborhood, and one evening I saw them dressed for some special occasion—dressed in a cloth that billowed from their bodies like the pink feathers floating above the legs of the strange birds on the playing cards. And in the marbles collected by my brother, there were pink and blue clouds changing as they sped across the floor, changing too in the light as I held them up to the window.

One evening, I sat watching the sunset in its pinks and blues. And as I sat, I felt the sunset as one thing, and myself as another. The cement sidewalk on which I sat was one thing. I was another, the same me. I knew at that moment, I could not be the sun, the hills, the color pink. I knew also that the world I could see was a world of change, and the world I could not see was inside me. Though some things would be pink, some would be blue, I would always be me. I sat in the sun and gazed at the hills.

* * *

When President Roosevelt Died

I could not believe it. How could our president, who was almost like God, die? How could he die and leave us with a war to finish? I asked my mother, repeatedly, "How did he die?"

Attempting to simplify her answer for a child's understanding, she replied each time, "He died from a terrible headache."

A headache! I knew what headaches were. I had already begun having headaches. Would I, too, die from a headache someday? Did I have to fear dying every time I had a headache?

I thought about these things as I watched a world in mourning: pictures of President Roosevelt on the front pages of newspapers, grave voices over the radio, hushed discussions of my grandfather and other adults, who gathered to grieve and worry together.

The plan was to gather in the living room of our house at a time when all other American families would gather, to form a circle, and silently remember and honor this great president, a fellow sufferer in this great and terrible war. A family from across the street was to join us, so there would be several people in this circle: my grandfather, my grandmother, my mother, Aunt Marie and Uncle Bill, cousin V.J., my brother Dick, me—and Freddie and his parents. I knew Freddie. He was a friend and playmate, and I was glad to have someone my age present at this somber occasion. Freddie would understand me. We would be together.

When the time came to gather, we formed the silent circle, holding hands and listening to a country holding still, a country hardly breathing. It was then that I looked up and saw Freddie. He was looking at me too; and some part of us that was not part of this collective grief—not a part of this war which was slowly and surely suffocating us—escaped, and ignited.

We began to giggle, quietly at first. But the more we tried to control our giggles, the more impossible it was to do so. The more ashamed we felt, the more intense were our giggles. Our shoulders shook, and our faces turned red with shame and the effort to make the giggles stop.

How could we do such a thing? This was a terrible thing, this president's death, this death which symbolized the war with its millions of deaths. How could we stand there, honoring this dead president, and laugh uncontrollably?

The moment of horror passed. The moment of terrible silence passed. But though we were never punished, the memory of shame lingered. The shame, and the guilt.

* * *

Victory Garden

We plowed the ground near Kansas City Plaza, dropping seeds like tiny buttons in straight black rows. Grandma Lizzie, in her starched sun bonnet, moved ahead. I followed her, the shadow of my bonnet bobbing over the soft dirt crumbs, the hot Kansas sun on my back. Earthworms, like shiny slick tubes, tunneled our work. We covered the seeds and hoped for corn, cucumbers, peas and squash. Carrots, beets, green beans and tomatoes.

I knew our city garden was not play. Those green things pushing up through the dirt would do more than feed us. They meant we counted on the war to end. They meant the return of soldiers, my father. Wild parades with people hanging out of windows of tall buildings, tossing a million bits of paper through the air.

For Grandma, they meant the return of her daughter and grandchildren to their own home, and her return to the farm waiting for her in the hills of western Kansas. Her own house, her own tomatoes.

* * *

About George Weber

Sometimes, after the war was over and we began living in our Wichita house, I would be outdoors playing, or just sitting by myself under the elm trees in the front yard, thinking about George Weber. George Weber was another person in my life, sort of an extra. There were my mother, my brother, my grandparents and me—and all the other people we lived with during the war years. And there was George Weber.

George Weber started coming, and we got used to him, like we got used to listening to Gabriel Heater on the radio, and collecting newspapers, and planting gardens that were supposed to make the war end. I don't remember anything George Weber ever said to me, but I do remember that he had big hands that showed where all the bones were, and a long skinny body that had to bend to where I was. He also had a big nose, not very much hair, and eyes that didn't seem to have any color at all.

That's about all I can remember really, except he brought us things. At least, he brought *me* things. One afternoon I woke up from my nap looking at a wooden doll cradle by my bed. It had blue and red flowers painted on it and was just the right size for my 'Daddy Doll' that my father had sent me from Hawaii. Hawaii was a spatter of little dots in the middle of a great blue part of the globe I would bring my mother to point out where Daddy was and where we lived. Though I could reach the two places with both my hands on the globe, I knew it was a long way and that I couldn't see my father until the war was over and all the soldiers had come home.

When George Weber started coming to see us, I stopped upsetting my mother by running up to any man with a uniform on, tugging his sleeve and insisting he was my father. George Weber didn't go to the war because he had a bad heart, and like flat feet, a bad heart kept you from going to war. Something else George Weber brought me one time was a beautiful pink dress made of a cloth that rustled when I walked. It had sleeves that puffed up and a blue furry ribbon going in and out down the front, and sashes that tied in a bow in the back. I had my picture taken in this same dress when the war was finally over and my father had come back. My father made the picture, and it won a prize in a photo contest.

George Weber took me places. One time, he came by on a Sunday morning and asked to take me to the park. I was sure my mother would not let me go because it had been raining and the ground and everything was all wet. But we went anyhow, and George Weber spread newspapers on the heavy swing seat so I could sit dry on it while he pushed me higher and higher. I wasn't afraid, though, because George Weber was there behind me, pushing me. I just couldn't fall. I did worry, though, that pushing my swing would make him throw up and have to go to the hospital, like my grandfather did when he had his first heart attack. But that didn't happen then.

Another time, George Weber took me to dinner at 'The Pink Elephant.' I had begged and begged to be taken to 'The Pink Elephant' ever since I heard my mother talking about it one time with her friend Margie. I loved to say the name over and over, "The Pink Elephant, The Pink Elephant," like there was something magical about the place—like the pillow my father sent my mother one Christmas from Hawaii. It was made of shiny slick cloth and was light blue, with dark blue silky strings all around. It had a map of Hawaii on one side, bigger than the spatters on the globe, with ladies in grass skirts and trees with all their branches and leaves at the top. I always took my naps with this pillow, and on hot afternoons I would lay my cheek against the smooth map of where my father was and sleep for a long time.

'The Pink Elephant' turned out to be an ordinary restaurant, but since it was a place for grownups, I was excited to be there anyhow. I tried to use my knife and fork like I was supposed to and not use my fingers to scoop the food onto my fork. I didn't even hide pieces of my chewed meat under my plate. That always upset everyone.

I really can't remember anything else about George Weber, except that he taught me to tie my shoes. It took a whole afternoon, but I learned how, tying my shoes every which way while George Weber explained again and again just how to loop one string and hold it with one hand, while you wrap the other string around the loop and make it loop too. George Weber was left-handed, and I still tie George Weber knots and bows, even though I am right-handed.

After the war, George Weber didn't come anymore; he just disappeared, first, and then he died. My mother told me about it a long time afterward. I wasn't sad, then. My father had come back and carried me on his shoulders around the yard, just like I'd planned. He had brought a big trunk of stuff from Hawaii and let my brother and me rummage through it. But I didn't like the guns much, and my brother got to wear the officer's hat.

We stopped planting gardens and saving newspapers and had moved away from my grandparents' house in Kansas City into a brick house in Wichita, where I had my own room with blue patterned wallpaper that I liked to look at whenever I was sick. My mother baked pies every day, and we went camping in Colorado in the summer. I got a new baby brother and played less with my dolls, even though I kept the wooden cradle George Weber gave me. I kept the pink dress too, even after I was too big to wear it. In summer, I took long naps in the basement of the brick house, the cool air making sweat on the asphalt tile floor, the blue satin pillow, cool under my cheek.

VIII

After the War

The end of the war and return of soldiers to their families did not necessarily mean a return to normalcy for many of us. Couples did not really know one another after four or more years apart, and many children did not know their fathers, who had suffered war horrors, the memory of which continued to plague them for many years. My own father's return, for which we had yearned so long and passionately, brought ambivalent feelings to my mother, my brother and me. It was at this time that I began to be closer to my mother, and Grandma Lizzie began to retreat into the background of my memory.

For her part, my mother had to face the disappointment that this knight in uniform was not interested in escorting her to military balls and treating her to restaurant dinners by candlelight. She had scrimped and saved throughout the war and was ready to cut loose, celebrate and have a good time. For my father, a good time meant backyard picnics, cooking on a new brick barbecue he had built, camping trips in Colorado, and adding another child to the family.

My adored brother Dick had to endure the strict military discipline and expectations of manliness from a father who called him a 'sissy' for having lived too long with a mother and sister. This was especially painful for Dick, who had considered himself the man of the family, as long as my father was away, even though we all acknowledged Grandpa John as the head of the household while we lived with our grandparents. And I, who had been spoiled by Grandma Lizzie, and fiercely defended by her (even though I was often in the wrong), could not get used to the reality of a flesh-and-blood father, who once forced me to eat a bowl of stewed plums, which I thought revolting, by making me sit at the table long into the evening after everyone else had finished and the dishes had been cleared, washed and put away.

"Mama, do I have to mind that man?" I was reported to have asked my mother. I was confused also by her frequent tears and my brother's moodiness. Our close friendship seemed to widen as he sought friends and activities outside the home. And I was absolutely forbidden to enter his room without permission, often hanging about outside his door to marvel at the delicate model airplanes built out of tissue paper and balsa wood that were hung from the ceiling. I continued to adore him, but he began to tease and patronize me, partly, I suppose, because I was younger and would not question his greater knowledge of the world.

In later years, Dick and I wondered why we had lived all the war years in Kansas City with Grandpa and Grandma Vesecky (with short residencies in Lincoln, Nebraska, and Topeka, where my mother, trying to escape the overbearing influence of our grandparents, had taken us), when my parents had actually bought a house in Wichita before the war. We speculated that my mother wanted to rent the house during that time, live with our grandparents and save the money for my father's hoped-for return. After the house on Mercier Street in Kansas City, the brick house on St. Clair in Wichita is the first house I can remember.

It was an ordinary little brick house with white trim, shaded by elms in the front yard. My mother kept a bed of old-fashioned flowers on either side of the front door—petunias and 'pinks,' marigolds and phlox. Inside were a living room, dining room, kitchen, bath and two bedrooms on the ground floor. Later, the full basement was made into a play room, laundry room and bedroom for my brother, all eventually floored with a brown asphalt tile flecked with white, gold and black. I still can recall the scent of those sweating tiles in the summer, when we played ping-pong downstairs, escaping the scorching heat.

I liked having my own room, though I often would become frightened by nightmares and sneak into my parents' bed in the middle of the night. The wallpaper in my room was blue and white, patterned so that if I looked at it one way there were flowers, and if I blurred my eyes the flowers became abstract designs.

We gradually began to get along as a family, probably because we all desperately wanted to *be* a family. Compromises were made. My mother bought a new slinky ball gown — powder blue jersey, cinched with a leather belt studded with glass 'jewels' — which she wore to a military ball, accompanied of course by my handsome father in full officer's uniform. My brother and I settled into our own rooms for the first time in our lives and began to enjoy a sense of security of having my father, whom I called "Daddy," at home. And Daddy got his camping trips in Colorado.

I believe it was on one of these trips that my brother Frank was conceived. Born March 19, 1948, he was named after my paternal grandfather, Franklin Daniel Fox. Though he was a skinny, rather homely baby, I loved him dearly and took on simple babysitting chores from the very beginning, holding him in a rocker and singing little nonsense rhymes to put him to sleep, and folding his diapers a special way for boy babies.

Many of my parents' siblings must have had the same notion of expanding their families, for a whole new tier of cousins were born around the time of my brother's birth: Thompson to Aunt Bing and Uncle Steve; Billy, to Aunt Marie and Uncle Bill; another John, "Johnnie," to Uncle Al and Aunt Betty. On my father's side came David, to Aunt Mary and Uncle Lawrence; and Steve (and later, Stan) to Aunt Ruth and Uncle Cleason. These cousins had been preceded during, and shortly after, the war years by Diane (Cooney), Kathy (Minter), Virginia "Gini" and later Susie (Emrich) and Georgie (Kathary), on the Fox side; and Stephanie (Vesecky), Stevie (Larson), and Connie (Vesecky) on the Vesecky side.

My sister Katy was not born until February 2, 1956, the family 'straggler,' whom we all adored and spoiled. I took care of her the first two years of her life, becoming more a second mom than a sister. Since she was nearly 16 years younger than I, who was in high school at the time, I really did not get to know her until she moved to Salisbury, Maryland, to attend the college where I was teaching at the time. We were close ever since, building on the bond we undoubtedly formed those first two years. She had been even closer to our brother Frank, who was tragically killed in a train accident in 1968. They had formed one set of siblings, sharing many of the same memories, as Dick and I had formed another. This lack of a common early history is something she and I lamented over the years.

Katy died of multiple illnesses and complications in 2007, only weeks before her 51st birthday. The grief wounds persist, and always will, as do those caused by the deaths of my two eldest children: Kirsten at age 9 and Brendan at age 23. As of this writing, our family has also lost cousins Stephanie Vesecky, Steve Minter, David Cooney and Hugh and Susie Emrich, as well as all of the aunts and uncles, including Aunt Eva, who died a few years ago at age 97. Most recently, my brother Dick, sister-in-law June and their son Jorn lost their daughter/sister, Cindy.

* * *

Such a large family on both sides inspired many holiday and summer gatherings, especially since most of us lived in Kansas, or at least in the wide prairie states from Texas to North Dakota. Memorial Day, July 4th and Thanksgiving were usually spent with Grandma and Grandpa Fox, along with aunts, uncles and cousins. On Thanksgiving Day, we impatiently awaited the presentation of the turkey and wonderful pumpkin and mincemeat pies prepared by Grandma Fox and her daughters, as well as the pies my mother contributed. We kids argued over who would get a drumstick, or the coveted wishbone. My cousin Hugh, whom we called 'Hughie,' was especially passionate, and insistent, about these issues.

Christmas was always reserved for the magical reunions with Grandma Lizzie and Grandpa John, who welcomed and embraced their sprawling family at their Timken farm. My brother Dick and I had been introduced to the farm one summer after the war. While we were snooping around the house, exploring, the telephone rang…and rang…and rang. Frantically looking around us, we followed the rings to the dining room, where we searched in vain for the telephone, only discovering later it was an old-fashioned brown box phone hanging on the wall. We were charmed by this odd telephone, and delightedly rang up neighbors with the hand crank, even though my grandparents were on a party line, and our conversations were listened to by half the county.

* * *

IX

The Farm

Whenever I dream of or think about a place I'd like to go back to, a place I'd like to reclaim, I think about the farm. My maternal grandparents' farm in west-central Kansas is always *the* farm in my memory—not *a* farm—and I cannot think of the farm without also remembering our Christmases there.

All of my mother's siblings and their families—along with my parents and my siblings—would make every effort to battle sudden blizzards in order to arrive at the Vesecky farm for Christmas Eve. As a child, I used to count the hills before the little town of Timken would come into view.

"It's just over the next hill," my mother assured us, and at some point, she would be right.

Just outside of town, bordering Walnut Creek, my grandparents' white frame farmhouse appeared. The two-story-high cedar tree snuggling next to the front porch beckoned with the colored outdoor lights my grandfather put up every year. Sometimes there would be snow, and we would drive carefully over the curved dirt road, actually a driveway that ended in the barnyard itself, park our luggage and package-laden car and race in to greet Grandma Lizzie and Grandpa John at the back door—the 'mud room' adjoining the warm and cozy kitchen. It was also the place my grandmother wintered-over her geraniums, growing tall and leggy as they strained against the cold window toward the weak winter sun.

I loved that farmhouse nearly as much as I loved my grandparents, and I loved exploring the rooms that seemed to hold so many surprises, yet remain so familiar. If we entered through the front door, instead of the mud room and kitchen, we hung up coats, hats and mittens on the oak valet with mirror that stood to the right of the entrance. Heat from the furnace below rose through a large floor vent in the middle of the hall between the parlor to the left and the dining room on the right.

After glancing into the parlor to make sure a recently cut cedar tree was braced in the corner, as usual, and as usual decorated with tinsel and colored balls, I would check the dining room to see if Grandma had set up her Christmas scene on top of the oak buffet, or sideboard, that matched the large oak table and chairs. She never failed to delight us with her display of incongruous items: nativity figures featuring the holy family, shepherds with their sheep, three wise men—along with Santa Claus and eight reindeer, Frosty the Snowman and snow globes—all floating upon a cloud of white cotton snow.

Next, we had to race through the hall closet, which magically turned into my grandparents' bedroom closet, out of which we burst in order to race through the hall to repeat the process, dodging adults who indulged us, though inevitably getting in *our* way.

Then there was the second floor. Sprinting up the stairway with its polished bannister, we checked out the bedrooms that once had belonged to my uncles Al and Steve, and to Aunt Marie and my mother. Al and Steve's room had the bonus of an attic closet, into which we bravely peered just far enough to be a bit spooked. My mother's room had a somewhat smaller closet and view of the vegetable garden. But Aunt Marie's room was the best. Though small, it opened onto a tiny balcony from which one could survey the front yard, the road to town and beyond, and the fields bordering the creek.

It was from Aunt Marie's room that some of us sometimes sneaked out of the house, when we were supposed to be snuggled into numerous feather beds Grandma had spread on the wood floors. Braving the night chill on the balcony, we (some of us) climbed down the lighted cedar tree, crept along the front porch and spied on our elders drinking bourbon and arguing politics into the night. These drinks, turned black by the iron in the farm's well water, held a mysterious fascination for us, especially since they accompanied such lively conversations. When it was just too cold to venture out of the house, we simply held our ears close to the warm floor vents in each bedroom, stifling giggles at the secrets we weren't supposed to hear.

(Unfortunately, more than one member of our family suffered from excessive alcohol consumption, and for some, it contributed to an early death, so my memories of this convivial joy are now accompanied by those of loss and grief.)

Mornings found at least a half-dozen of us lined up outside the single bathroom, waiting our turns at the toilet and wash basin. Though there was a claw foot iron and porcelain tub, we used it only occasionally—never in the morning—relying on sponge baths and tooth brushing for daily hygiene.

Breakfasts were eaten in shifts, with some of us packed into the wooden booth alcove in the kitchen, and some of us at the oak dining table with the adults, where we were expected to watch our manners, eat with silver plate flatware on Grandma's Bohemian china, daintily nibbling soft-boiled eggs and—my favorite—poppy seed koláches baked by one of my great-aunts.

These koláches, delicious pastries filled with poppy seed or prunes, were kept in the pantry in a green and brown speckled crock with a lid, which we lifted several times a day in order to sneak extras. Sometimes, the crock was empty, and we were left with the teasing scent of absent koláches — and maybe a thousand cookies past. I have this crock today, and the sweet, slightly musty scent brings back the pantry at the farm and all its poignant memories.

After breakfast, we scattered — some of us to join an improvised hockey game on the iced-over Walnut Creek. It didn't matter whether or not we had skates. We skittered across the ice, chasing a makeshift puck, shouting over dubious goals. Uncle Steve once slipped on the ice, spraining his wrist. Aside from the pain it caused him, it also hampered his performance at the barbecue, where he usually stood a shivering watch over the sizzling precious choice steaks he had brought from Texas.

If there was snow, we all — adults included — took turns sledding down the hill across the road, over the frozen creek, and if we were lucky, halfway up the other side. Only our persistently freezing toes and fingers forced us to retreat inside the farmhouse, lay our wet mittens and leggings on the large hall vent and seek out hot chocolate — and maybe a poker game featuring colored toothpicks instead of chips. Poker games were marathons at the farm, and we often took over a hand while someone wrapped last minute packages, helped with the cooking, or returned to the sledding in the crisp, clean air outdoors.

What went on in the kitchen was close to a miracle, considering the traffic in and out with people checking on the cooking and wonderful smells. The 'staff' rotated among my aunts and mother—and of course, Grandma Lizzie, who ran the kitchen, ordering everyone around, scolding us in Czech. Some of the specialties were orchestrated by whoever brought the ingredients—like the red snapper from Kansas City, purchased and prepared by Aunt Marie and Uncle Bill for Christmas Eve. Or the Texas steaks Uncle Steve brought from Dallas and lovingly grilled outdoors. Or the pies my mother turned out—cherry, pumpkin, mincemeat. Uncle Bill tended bar, and Aunt Bing supervised the setting of tables.

But Grandma handled the goose, turkey—or ducks—from start to finish. If the bird or birds of choice were her own, she personally played the executioner, then dressed them out, ready for baking. Her stove, originally wood-burning, had been converted to gas, and the deep oven swallowed the bird, which was inspected several times an hour in case it needed basting with the fat rising up around it. On the burners sizzled the mushrooms and giblets for gravy, while potatoes boiled until ready for mashing—also Grandma's province. She attacked the tender white potatoes with a masher, all the while pouring in cream and spooning butter that melted as soon as it dropped into the mound, which fluffed up, filling the large mixing bowl.

One Christmas, as we hungrily made final preparations for the presentation of the Christmas goose and all its trimmings, we were visited by some of our distant Czech relatives, who just 'happened' to drop by at dinner time.

"Can we hold dinner awhile?" went the word to the kitchen, as we politely ushered into the parlor whiskered great uncles, kerchiefed great aunts—and second or third cousins we had never seen before—offering them tea, or maybe a glass of sherry.

They must have known we were ready to sit down to our Christmas dinner, but on they sat, and sat—mischievously stalling their departure, chatting with Grandpa John in Czech or German—as the rest of us groaned inwardly, matching their talk with the rumblings of our stomachs. Salivating over the delicious aromas coming from the kitchen, we kids milled around impatiently.

"When are they going to leave?" we complained to one another in the hallway. "And what about the goose—won't it be overcooked?"

At last, the disappointed relatives filed out of the warm and cozy farmhouse with its cooking smells and impatient gathering, and we all crowded around the tables set in the dining room and strung out across the entrance hall, where at last we ate our fill, the kids sipping 'real' Mogen David wine from Grandma Lizzie's fancy juice glasses.

The part of the farm I have not yet mentioned is the cellar, or basement, since the cellar was officially the outdoor storm cellar into which we scurried for shelter during the violent summer storms. The basement, which both frightened and intrigued me, was the dark, cavernous belly of the house. It was the storage area for Grandma's jars of home canning on shelves covering one wall of the cellar and stocked with the fruits and veggies of her labor. From her summer garden, she canned tomatoes, tomato sauce, 'chow-chow' relish, horseradish, beans, peas and carrots. She put up—from the grocer, or neighboring farms—applesauce, pears, apricots, cherries, and plums.

At Christmas time—or during summer visits—I would often be sent below to find, and pluck off the shelf, preserved food for dinner. Descending into that darkness required courage, and more light than was afforded by the few bare light bulbs dangling on cords from the ceiling. Keeping a sharp eye out for spiders, I would quickly lift the dusty jars off the shelves, and as quickly ascend the stairs again to light and safety.

Grandma's washing machine and wringer were also in the basement, along with the clean smell of her homemade lye soap, hardening, as always, in trays for cutting. Indoor lines were strung close to the ceiling, drying the laundry with heat from the great boiler furnace in the center of the cellar. The furnace rumbled throughout the winter days—and dozed quietly at night when sleepers snuggled under down comforters and on top of featherbeds, covering the floors where we kids slept.

The only occasion when I wasn't wary of the basement was when Uncle Steve, requiring an assistant for organizing his yearly *Day After Christmas Grab Bag*, chose me to help him put numbers on everyone's unwanted white elephants and print the same numbers on little slips of paper to be drawn from a hat that evening. The day after Christmas was always something of a letdown for us. Presents had been opened, most of the special food had been eaten and the endless poker games began to lose their charm. But most of us didn't yet want to leave the cozy camaraderie we were enjoying. So, Uncle Steve invented the *Grab Bag*, which, in many ways, turned out to be more fun than the presents on Christmas night. Someone once put a bag of plastic orange and black Halloween witches into the grab bag—and they turned up as a booby prize that circulated among us, year after year. At a family reunion many years ago, we repeated the *grab bag*. Among the prizes was one surviving black plastic witch.

But the basement with its monstrous furnace established its true value, when upstairs we took turns standing on the large metal grate in the hall—out of which the precious heat burst forth to warm us all. Never in my life have I felt so secure—and so at peace—as when I stood on the grated vent with my grandfather behind me, feeling his belt buckle against my back, his warm breath on the top of my head, and his strong arms holding me.

X

Two Christmas Portraits

Joy in Small Packages

I've been thinking lately of my Uncle Frank—that is, my mother's uncle, making him great-uncle Frank. He *was* great. Though small and wiry, he packed power and wit, and more than a bit of orneriness, into his small frame. An immense energy seemed to vibrate outward to the tips of his once flaming red hair.

Married to my great-aunt Mary, a large and buxom woman with twice his girth, Uncle Frank balanced her attempts to govern him with jollity and humor. Winking at us cousins, visiting at Christmas during the yearly gathering of my mother's siblings and their families at the farm, Uncle Frank would whisk out his fiddle and start to play. Such power in those short, stubby fingers, as they deftly marched across the strings, his bow dancing polkas, waltzes and Czech folk tunes by the score.

"More!" we cried, joining in the conspiracy to frustrate frowning Aunt Mary, who cajoled: "Frank, you have to slosh the pigs!" or "What about those two fat hens? You promised to wring their necks for plucking!"

She reminded me of the Queen of Hearts in *Alice in Wonderland*: square-built and humorless. Not unkind, she nevertheless was not our favorite, and she knew it.

I liked to think Uncle Frank was one of Santa's wily elves that we kept believing in, Christmas after Christmas. We wanted to immortalize him. I still can hear the scrape and drag of his bow upon the fiddle. Still, I see his wild hair, his crafty grin.

Aunt Marie At Christmastime

When she was little, she was called "Middie," her own pronunciation of her name, since she could not yet manage *r's*; and "Middie" she was called by family until even that nickname got shortened to "Mid," and later for her nieces and nephews, "Aunt Mid." I cannot think of Christmas without sifting through memories of Aunt Mid. Petite with large brown eyes and brown hair worn short with bangs, she was enthusiastic, imaginative and ready for fun. My younger brother Frank and I used to hope our folks would go on one of my father's business trips just before Christmas so we could be taken to Aunt Mid and Uncle Bill's, where there was always a bustle of excitement.

One year, they and our cousins Stevie and Billy had just returned from Sanibel Island, Florida. Charmed by the wealth of seashells on the beaches, they collected buckets of these exotic treasures—exotic to Kansans, many of whom had never seen the sea—and brought the shells home. Aunt Mid set up a Christmas workshop, where glue, pipe cleaners, paint and glitter turned the shells into ornaments that we all thought were extraordinary: little shell dolls with pipe cleaner arms and legs, shell Santas with tiny shell caps painted red. Frank and I participated in these transformations, and Aunt Mid let us use our imaginations to produce clumsy interpretations of her more skillful creations.

Another pre-Christmas visit to Aunt Mid's introduced me to outdoor skating. Borrowing a pair of Uncle Bill's hockey skates and layering on two or three pairs of socks, I was able to skim over the ice of a neighborhood pond with more grace than I had mustered with figure skates on an indoor rink back home. Between turns on the ice, we sipped hot chocolate next to a bonfire near the pond. We were in Independence, Missouri, but I thought I was in heaven.

At the farm, Aunt Mid was always at the center of festivities—concocting gourmet *hors d'oeuvres* and telling stories, snorting at her own jokes, and swilling a black bourbon drink at the same time. All my aunts and uncles, along with my parents and grandparents, indulged in these black cocktails. They didn't seem to mind the color, and I always suspected the bourbon drinks tasted better than the iron-stained water alone, which we gulped down without giving it a chance to make us retch.

On Christmas Eve, we gathered in the tiny parlor, where a scraggly cedar tree festooned with tinsel and colored balls seemed to be supported by piles of gifts to be opened the next morning, and later on Christmas night, after the Veseckys from Dallas had arrived. Aunt Marie and Uncle Bill led us in the singing of carols. He squeezed out the notes on a little concertina Aunt Mid had given him one Christmas, while she curled herself into a ball, catlike, sometimes closing her eyes, as they harmonized *Silent Night.* Her mouth made the *O* sounds the same way a cherub-faced boy sang carols at our morning songfest in grade school. He stole my heart, and I daydreamed someday marrying him and having angel-faced children who looked just like him.

But Aunt Mid could be bossy too, ordering everyone around to complete chores and run errands. She was like Grandma Lizzie in this respect. We even sometimes teased her by calling her "Uncle Mid," and our uncle, "Aunt Bill." One year, we decided to have some fun by hiding her Dior black dress, then begging her to model it for us. She returned from the closet, distraught.

"My designer dress is gone!" she announced, perplexed.

We enjoyed her plight, but feigning sympathy, we frantically 'searched' the house with her before someone furtively returned the dress to the closet. The jig was up when she was urged to look for it there just one more time.

One Christmas, she and Uncle Bill disappeared while we were all absorbed in one of our marathon poker games, warming up after an afternoon of sledding or riding old Snowball at great-uncle Frank's farm. Gradually, we began to notice their absence. Just as our curiosity was peaking, Aunt Mid and Uncle Bill emerged from the cellar. Wrapped in a white sheet cinched with old chains and locks, Uncle Bill stood mutely with his jaws held together by a white napkin tied in a knot above his head, a sorrowful expression on his face.

"Marley's Ghost!" we laughed, impressed with the transformation. Aunt Marie stood quietly by his side, sweetly smiling her little crooked smile, made crooked from a small scar caused by the kick of a horse in her childhood. Dressed in another white sheet, a tinseled coat hanger halo askew above her head, she was, and always has been for me, the true ghost of Christmas past.[†]

[†] To anyone reading these Christmas stories, it would seem they could be companions for Grandma Moses's naive paintings, dripping with nostalgia — and in some way, they are — frozen in a bygone age, even within our own lifetimes.

XI

Epilogue

I had not been back for many years, not since that last Christmas at the farm when my grandmother was still alive, Grandpa John having died of a heart attack two years before. We all had tried to revive the warmth and good times of earlier days, but we knew the end of an era was at hand.

Now I wanted my (then) eight-year-old son Franklin, named for, and in memory of, my brother Frank, to see where his grandmother grew up, where his great-grandparents had lived and farmed. And where his mother, visiting at Christmas and during summer vacations, had tried to fit into this tiny Czech community—also trying clumsily to master a few Czech phrases with which to greet the town folk, most of whom were distant relatives. In later years, I found out the phrase we were taught was a Czech greeting was really translated as, "Shut your mouth!" Another example of mischievous Czech humor.

The dusty road leading from town crossed a one-lane bridge over what used to be Walnut Creek, now completely dried up—from irrigation, I suppose, and the more and more frequent droughts. A ledge formed what was once a little waterfall, now only a crumbling dry rock wall. My brother Frank and I used to play there to cool off on hot summer afternoons, and during one of these visits, we encountered and adopted a wonderful, loyal Brittany spaniel we named 'Timmy.'

Already disappointed as we drove into the entrance to the Vesecky farm, I was shocked that the original farmhouse had vanished. In its place stood a modern ranch-style house—so out of place, so wrong. I knew that the farm had been sold, after my grandmother's death, in order to pay off the heavily mortgaged property, but somehow, I expected to at least see the farmhouse, still standing.

Inquiries revealed that the house had been sold and moved into the town of Timken. Determined, I resolved to track it down. At least I could show my son the house, which I hoped would be the same as I remembered it.

Immediately upon locating it, I again was disappointed. Instead of an open front porch, where my grandfather and I had sat on summer nights, naming the stars—and where my cousins had scrambled down from the little balcony off Aunt Mid's room—there was a glassed-in porch—so small, it seemed, so enclosed. A knock at the door brought a young girl, who told us she was babysitting.

"Who owns this house now?" I asked her, also asking if we might come in and look around. "I want to show my son where his great-grandparents lived," I explained. Hesitant, she stood aside to let us enter.

Room by room, I led Franklin through the house, explaining how it used to look, explaining how we sat in the parlor, opening Christmas gifts, laughing at the post-Christmas grab-bag jokes. How we ate Christmas dinners on tables overflowing into the hall. How we slid down the polished bannister from the hall linking bedrooms that once had belonged to my uncles, my aunt, my mother.

We stayed as long as it was polite to do so. How small it all seemed now, how painfully altered. We said goodbye and thank you on the step down from the front porch.

"At least," I told Franklin, "the house belongs to someone named Kraisinger. That was Grandma's maiden name."

At least, I thought to myself as we climbed back into the VW camper, *at least surrounding the house were the deep beds of color: red, orange, yellow, purple — dozens and dozens of Grandma Lizzie's cherished zinnias.*

There was only one more stop to make before leaving the town, if not its memories, behind.

"I'll bet you don't know who I am!" I challenged Eddie, who eyed me with bulging pale blue eyes behind thick glasses—the same eyes that had welcomed my cousins and me as we crowded into Eddie's Timken store for ice cream so many years ago. As he scanned my face, I grinned, certain the years would mask my identity.

"You're Fern's girl," he replied, without hesitation. Astonished, I wondered which of my features had given me away, yoking me, a stranger to him now, to my mother, a cousin he had known so well. *The hint of Slavic cheekbones?* Not my blond hair; my mother's was a riotous red. *The long legs?* He couldn't see mine, hidden behind the counter.

It must have been the smile that betrayed me—the smile, a near replica of my mother's. Both pleased and shocked by Eddie's recognition, I marveled at the genetics that linked me so inevitably to my mother. Fern's girl.

I mused also that I was similarly linked to my father and his forebears. Then, as if in lucid dream, my selfhood seemed to funnel out of me. As if through a reverse telescope, I saw far back into the past, beyond my mother and grandmother, beyond my great grandmothers. I saw the red hair fly past, like poppies in the wind. I saw the long legs running through wheat fields in another land. I saw the smile, manifested over hundreds, if not thousands, of years, linking me not only to my mother, but to my human kind, through generations of change that eventually came to be me, Fern's girl.

Photo Gallery

Vesecky family farm

Vesecky grandparents, John and Elizabeth (Lizzie)

Vesecky Family: 1st row: Lizzie and John. 2nd row, left to right: Steve, Marie, Fern, Al

Fox grandparents, Frank and Cora

Fox Family: 1st row, left to right: Ruth, Eva, (Fern, pregnant with me, brother Dick in front), Mary, behind, Dick, Grandma Fox (Cora), Genevieve. 2nd row, left to right: Don (my father), Cleason ('C.K.', Ruth's husband), Lawrence (Mary's husband), 'Bud' (Genevieve's husband)

Fox sisters, left to right: Eva, Mary, Ruth and Genevieve

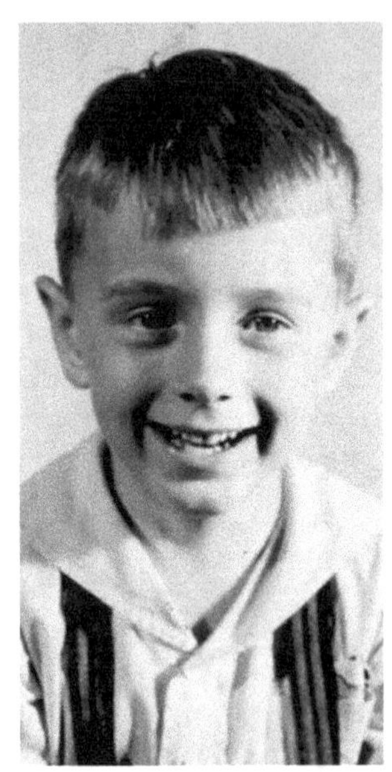

Brother Dick

Author, age 1

My father, Don Fox

My mother, Fern Vesecky Fox

My brother Frank at Walnut Creek, near the Vesecky Farm

Author's Note

I include two of the following appendices, written by my grandfather Vesecky, not only because they add fullness to my own story, but especially in the case of the second — a radio address in 1936 — they evidence wisdom gained over his life of study, understanding and courage. The radio address itself is not just perceptive and wise, if idealistic, but shockingly prescient, given it was written over eighty years ago. Its insights and premonitions are as relevant today as they were in 1936, and its progressive ideas are sound.

One summer when I was about 12 or 13, while rocking in creaky armchairs with him on the front porch of the farm, I was so taken by his expansive wisdom that I asked Grandpa Vesecky why he had never run for president. His answer, in all humility, was, "Because I am not a natural born citizen of the United States."

Appendix I

Personal History of John Vesecky
(By John Vesecky)

I was born in Velka Ves, Cechy, May 13, 1879. My father's name was Stephan Vesecky and Mother's name, before her marriage, was Augusta Lhotka. My mother's home village was Vrackovice. My father and his father before him were small land holders and farmers. My mother's father was a weaver by trade, and as was usual at that time, farmed a small patch of ground in order to help out with living expenses.

My father was a liberal and more or less a rebel against the Austrian rule. He did everything that he could to keep from being drafted into the army because he hated militarism and all that it stood for. When the oldest boy Anton was nearing the age when he might be enrolled in the Army, father and mother decided to sell out their land and other property and move to America, where their boys would not have to serve three of their best years in the army, and then all the rest of their lives kowtow to every petty official.

I was the youngest of three boys and two girls that composed our family in the spring of 1880, when my parents decided to immigrate to the United States. The oldest boy Anton, then about 16 years of age, Marie, Frances, Frank and John (myself) in the order named and my parents and paternal grandmother made up the family at that time. As I was only a year old at the time, we crossed the ocean, I do not remember anything about the trip. I was told that I learned to walk on the ship, so that I really should have a good pair of sea legs.

We left Europe through the German port of Bremen, crossed on one of the early slow steamers to Baltimore and then took the train to Chicago, where Father's brother had a tailor shop. We lived in Chicago for two years. My next sister Christine was born in that city. Father worked in the boiler factory most of the time while we lived in Chicago, but he was never satisfied there. He was a farmer and longed for the land. In the spring of 1882, Father and a neighbor, Frank Stejskal, each bought out a half interest in a 160-acre homestead one-half mile south of what is now Timken, Kansas.

The land was poor, hilly, and part of it was very rocky. The house consisted of two small rooms dug out of the side of a rocky hill, walled out with small pick-up rocks and crudely plastered with magnesia. The roof was made of a log ridge pole, creek pole rafters, overlaid with a layer of small willow twigs, and that all covered with magnesia dirt. The floor was of packed clay. It never had to be scrubbed, but certainly had to be swept often, in order to keep it free from dust. We used one of the rooms for some time, and the Stejskal family used the other. As soon as possible, Father built a sod house on our half of the 160 acres so that both our families had a little more room. I do not remember anything of our life in Chicago, nor of the train ride to Great Bend, which was our closest railroad town, nor of the 30-mile ride cross-country in a lumber wagon from Great Bend to the farm, but the first night in our new home will stay with me forever. It seemed to me that the willows on the roof were full of terrible animals which made noises all night. Later, I found out that the noises were made by crickets which had made the willow ceiling their nightly concert hall.

The next few years were happy years for me, in spite of the absence of any luxuries and a shortage of the necessities of life. Because money was so scarce, Father and my oldest brother, and part of the time my two older sisters, helped out the family income by 'working out'—the sisters in town and father and brother on farms. Mother and the younger children took care of the yoke of Texas steers which father broke to work, and of the cattle and chickens. My first regular job was herding a sow and her litter of pigs, and watching that they did not stray away, or eat a watermelon that I was growing in a small draw. Even then I showed the Union spirit, because when once father called for me to go and drive the cattle out of the corn, I calmly answered that my job was to herd the pigs, and that is what I would do. Of course, I learned as soon as Dad drove the cattle out of the corn, that my labor union was not strong enough to save me from a good strapping and that it was best to obey those in authority.

During the time we lived on the farm near Timken, we had a small Indian scare. Some of the Indians that the government had moved from the Dakotas to the Indian Territory (now Oklahoma) left their reservation and started cross-country back to their home in the north. They got as far as Ness City about 50 miles west of Timken, where the soldiers from Ft. Hays rounded them up and took them back to the reservation. Neighbor Stejskal had his only cow stolen during the time we lived on the next 80, and his little boy Frank, about three years old, was lost for two or three days out on the prairies. The whole countryside was out hunting for him until he was found about three miles from home.

In 1885, father bought out a pre-emption claim about seven miles south of Timken and we moved there that fall. There, we again had to live in a stone-walled bank house facing to the east. We no more than got well settled, when the terrible snowstorm of 1886 came on. For two days, father could not go out to feed nor water the cattle, and when the storm finally stopped, he had to climb out of a small window on a level with the ground on the south side and shovel a path to the door, because it opened outward, and the snow was drifted as high as the roof. For two weeks, we used candles poured into a beer bottle form with string. That spring I started to go to school, whenever the weather was so that mother would trust me out on the road to school.

Schooling was a side-line those days. As we had no fences, my older brother Frank, and later my younger sisters, and I had to take turns about herding the cattle and going to school. Since the term of school usually consisted of five or six months, attending school every second day did not give us an even chance with the children of some of the "Yankee" settlers, most of whom had fenced pastures which could be used in winter and in bad weather, so that their children could go to school every day during the short school terms. There were four Czech families settled close together—Pivonka, Brazda, Chlumsky and we (us). Most of the time we and the Pivonka children were the only Czech children attending the school, the rest being all Yankee or Irish, as some of our folks called them. With only a few Bohemians, as we were called, in school, we did not have any bed of roses during the first two terms of school that I attended. As soon as we had mastered the English language and wore off our inferiority complex, we were able to hold our own against any combination of

Irish in school. One of the advantages that I had in school, was that there were only a few of us Czechs, so I had to learn to use the English language and to take my own part and fight out my own battles. Another advantage was the Literary Society that met in our school house every second week during every winter. Ours was one of the outstanding literary and debating societies in two counties, and really educated people took part in the literary programs and in the debates. I was not over twelve years old when I took part in my first debate, and the training I received in those debates stood me in good stead all my life.

My father died in the first flu epidemic, then known as 'La Grippe' in the spring of 1890. I was sick for about a month at that time also, but finally got well and strong again. My youngest sister Anna was only a year old when father died. The oldest boy Anton took charge of the farm and managed it with the help of the rest of us until he got married in the spring of 1893. After Anton got married, Frank and I were the only men left to work the farm, so thinking that I had learning enough for a farmer, I quit school and did not go to school again until the winter of 1896-97, when I managed to get time to go to school one month.

The next winter I planned to go all winter, but just as school was to open, Frank, sister Christine and I were getting some corn from shocks on the field to feed our hogs before we got it all husked. Frank was driving, standing in the front of the wagon. I reached under his arm to get a shotgun which was lying in the bottom of the wagon. The gun was loaded and went off accidentally and the whole load drove through my brother's arm. By a miracle, the shot, wad and a part of the coat went between the muscle and the arm bone, so that my brother's arm, outside of a large scar, is as good as ever. It was some time before he was able to help with the work, so I had to put off going to school until he could take care of some of the work on the farm.

At the close of that term of school, I took in a six-weeks Normal Institute in LaCrosse, the county seat town, received a third-grade teacher's certificate, and that winter I taught my first term of country school. It was not all smooth sailing even then. There was at that time a deep-rooted prejudice among most of the so-called natives against the foreigners, as they called us, and we had to overcome that before they would concede Czech equality and quit discriminating against our nationality when it came to hiring teachers.

One of the greatest influences in my life was the custom in my home of mother, my aunt, or some other member of the family who could read Czech, reading out loud of an evening. When I was 10 years old, Father gave me a copy of the Czech weekly, *Pokrok Zapadu,* helped me read the heading once, and ordered me to learn to name all the letters and read the name in other parts of the paper before I went to bed. I had, already at that time, acquired the reading habit, because of the custom of reading out loud in our home. In a short time, I could read both Czech and English, and read everything I could get to read. After my brother was married, he moved to a rented farm that belonged to the county Superintendent of Schools. There, while I helped him with his farm work, I found a treasure of books on all subjects— history, exploration, education, fiction and even medicine—and I believe that I read every page of all the books I found there. That is what really made up my mind for me to go to school again (after being out for three years).

In the spring of 1899, I attended Central Normal College in Great Bend, Kansas, for one semester. I taught school that winter again, and the next fall, 1900, I enrolled as a freshman in the Kansas State College in Manhattan. Because of short crops, I had to teach school again the next winter. In 1902, I attended another spring term in Central Normal College and graduated from a two-year course at the close of the semester.

For the next five years, I operated a country store with my brother-in-law, J.N. Pivonka, in Timken, Kansas, during the summer and taught school during the winter, until I was married to Elizabeth Kraisinger on June 2, 1907. The next year, I sold my interest in the store to my brother-in-law and took up farming during the summer and again taught school during the winter. All my life, I had either helped my parents work their farm or taught country schools among farmers or farmed on my own hook. When I was but a small boy, I used to attend the meetings of the Farmers Alliance in our school house, and later, the meetings of the Populist Party, which was the outgrowth of the Alliance movement. With this background, it was but natural that I joined the Farmers Union soon after it was organized in the Timken locality, and that I took from the first a prominent part in the Union activities in my neighborhood. I was then teaching the upper room of the Timken grade school. The Union local met in my room every second Saturday afternoon. When it was decided to organize a cooperative grain elevator, John Oborny and I were sent to Hutchinson to run the elevator from an old-line company, and I was selected to run the elevator as manager. I managed the elevator until the winter of 1926.

In the spring of that year, I was elected as President and Executive Officer of the South West Cooperative Wheat Growers Association, with permanent headquarters in the Board of Trade Building in Kansas City, Missouri. This cooperative organization was the sales agency of the Kansas, Oklahoma, Colorado and Nebraska wheat pools. It and its cooperating pools had a great future before them, if our farmers but had then the experience in managing large-size cooperatives that they have now. As it was, because of personal ambitions of some of the state officials, inexperienced personnel and the wrong kind of government interference, the pool never did do the work that we the founders hoped it would do, and in 1933, it was absorbed, together with other grain cooperatives in the Farmers National Grain Corporation. I was the president of the sales agency since its organization, and for the last five years, also of the Kansas Wheat Pool for about three months. In the spring of 1934, I held the position of Appraiser for the Wichita Bank for Cooperatives, but because I could not swallow the dictatorial orders of the higher ups in Washington, I resigned in May, and in June I went back to my farm a half-mile north of Timken, after an absence of eight years.

Contrary to what some people believe, officers of farmers organizations do not get rich on their salaries. I came back to my farm with only about two hundred dollars in money and no implements nor livestock. As you probably remember, this was in the worst dust storm year Kansas has ever had. We had no crop that year, nor the next — nor any year since then, except on irrigated land. Many days, we had to have the lights on during the whole day and our cattle in the barn because they could not find anything to eat that was not covered with dust.

In the fall of 1934, I was elected as delegate to the National Convention of the Farmers Union, which was held in Sioux Falls, S.D., and that winter I served as legislative representative or lobbyist in Topeka, for the Committee of Kansas Farm Organizations. That committee is composed of the State Grange, State Farm Bureau, State Farmers Union and all the statewide cooperative organizations in Kansas. Its purpose is to look out for the combined interests of Kansas farmers. In October 1935, I was elected president of the Kansas Farmers Union, and was reelected without opposition in 1936 and 1937. In November of 1936, I was unanimously elected vice president of the National Farmers Union, and in 1937, at the Oklahoma City convention, I was without opposition elected national president of the Farmers Union and was unanimously reelected to that position in 1938; and again, in Omaha this November 22nd, (1939).

My Czech heritage of love of liberty and democracy, and the inbred hate of militarism and autocracy, together with a large slice of Slavic idealism (which are some of the great gifts that our people have brought to this their new home), made it inevitable that I would join the Farmers Union, which is at present, I believe, the greatest exponent of human rights and especially of the rights of the lower one-third of our population in the United States. During the more than 25 years that I have been a member of the Farmers Union, it has had its ups and downs in the number of members, but it has always battled for equal opportunities for our farmers and for equity and justice to all. I hope that by organizing our farmers into the Farmers Union and educating them in such things, as they must know in order to better understand their privileges and also their due rights as American citizens, we can make secure those rights and privileges to all our citizens. By building farmers' cooperative business organizations and helping our city brethren build cooperatives in the cities, we hope to so modify the system of distribution, so as to assure both the farmers and the city dwellers fair exchange value for the result of their toil, and an opportunity to keep and enjoy the blessings secured for us by the constitution of the United States of America.

In all my travels over the United States, I have always publicly proclaimed my Czech ancestry, and as a result, I have had the pleasure of meeting with Czech folks on almost every trip. Although I am greatly pleased to note the many folks of my nationality who fill important positions in the Farmers Union and in the public life of this nation, still I am more pleased at the general high level of intelligence of all the Czechs that I meet and their practically universal devotion to their new home and to the principles of equality, liberty and democracy. I am also greatly encouraged by the understanding of the Czech people and the sympathy for their brave fight for liberty and democracy (which I have found among Americans of other than Czech ancestry). We Czechs in America have a debt of gratitude to repay the patriots in the Nazi-oppressed land of our birth for the wonderful showing they made in Czechoslovakia during the few years of its regained freedom. The results they have shown and the progress they have made in everything that makes for human happiness has been of great value in removing the prejudices against which we older folks had to contend upon our entry into public life in many parts of this country.

There are a few short statements that I have forgotten to put into their proper place. The Vesecky family consisted of Father and Mother, three boys and five girls. The oldest son Anton and two of the daughters (Marie and Anna) are now dead. Father died in 1890, and Mother died in 1906. Frances (now Mrs. J.N. Pivonka) lives in Dighton, Kansas. Frank lives in Timken. Antonia (now Mrs. E.H. Kaufman) lives in Pawnee Rock. Christine (now Mrs. George Hamrdla) lives now in LaCrosse, Kansas, and my wife, I and our youngest daughter Marie keep our legal residence on our small farm near Timken, just about a mile north of our first home in Kansas. We were blessed with four children. Albert and Stephen, both married, now live in Kansas City. Ferne, my oldest daughter, is married and lives in Wichita, and the youngest, Marie, now 22 years old, is still single and is living with us in Salina, Kansas, where we are making our home while I am president of the National Farmers Union. My wife and I are planning on going back to the farm as soon as my services are no more needed as the head of the Farmers Union.

Two of my sisters, Christine and Antonia, also taught school for several years. One of my boys, Stephen, graduated from the Kansas State College in Manhattan, and my other three children and all the in-laws have been students or are graduates from the same college. I am not saying this to brag, as there are large numbers of Czech boys and girls who are now students in our leading colleges and universities. I am saying this because I feel it is one of the best things we can do, both for our children and for our oppressed brothers and sisters across the ocean. By making it possible for our children to take their rightful place among the best of America, their new home, we are greatly aiding our folks in Czechoslovakia in their battle against absorption into the all-engulfing Nazi Pan Germanism. By showing that Czech culture and the Czech people are really worth saving, we can all do our bit to help regain Czech independence.

Appendix II

Radio address of John Vesecky, President, National Farmers Union over NBC, December 31, 1936:

The Age of Paradoxes

I am taking as the title of my today's talk, the many crazy things that people of the world and we ourselves in America have been doing during the last two decades. This is indeed the Age of Paradoxes.

Beginning with the World War down to the present day, it seems that we are trying to approach every problem by working from the opposite direction. Some of the things we do, do not have any more foundation in judgment or reason than the old saying which is current in many of the countries in Europe that, "If you want to cure a headache, the best thing to do is to put a cabbage leaf on the heel."

Over 20 years ago, we entered the World War with the avowed purpose of fighting a war to end all wars, yet ever since that time, the world has been in continual turmoil until now, 20 years later, every nation of the world is using most of its resources to build great armaments and all of its inventive genius to invent more horrible, more thorough methods of exterminating the human race.

We also fought the World War for the purpose of making the world "safe for democracy," yet today there are far more dictatorships in the world than at any time during the last 100 years, and the people of all nations, including our own, have surrendered far more of their liberties than they perhaps themselves realize. Even at the close of the war fought to save the world for democracy, the allied nations, in order to assure democracy, assumed dictatorial powers over the conquered nations.

We, in America, compelled our citizens even to borrow money to buy billions of dollars' worth of Liberty Bonds as a patriotic duty in order to win the war. We loaned a large part of the money to foreign nations and later, through deflation, compelled our citizens of small means to sell their Liberty Bonds, sometimes as low as 80 percent of the par value. Then, on top of that, because foreign nations have defaulted on payments of their bonds and interest, our own people must now pay the interest and principal of the bonds which they had bought once with the hope of assuring permanent peace to the world.

During the war, we urged our farmers to increase production of feed and fiber. We even went so far as to urge them to plant wheat, cotton and other crops in their front and back yards, to mortgage their farms to buy power machinery in order to produce more food and fiber. Then, after the war, we permitted a coterie of bankers to deliberately deflate our currency and call all loans in, that way bankrupting millions of our farmers and small business men, all in the name of bringing America back to normalcy. And now, we farmers are being criticized for breaking out too much land and buying too much machinery, and as a consequence producing too much.

We are afraid to trust Congress, which is responsible to the people, with its constitutional right to coin money and regulate the value thereof, but we delegate this same important power to banks and bankers who are not responsible to anyone except to their own stockholders, and to them but very little.

Millions of people are digging in the hills, freezing in the Arctic and roasting in the torrid regions, mining gold and silver. Our government buys this gold and silver and then buries it in the ground again so that nobody can see it or use it.

Through our uneconomic system of distribution, we displaced millions of workers in our factories, mines, offices and on our farms and then we grumble because of the cost of the PWA, WPA, FSA and other relief agencies which are necessary in order to take care of the millions thus thrown out of employment.

We have millions of half-fed, half-clothed people and still we are trying to bring prosperity back to our people—trying to clothe and feed them by curtailing productions of the very things they need.

Some of our "captains of industry" spent their lifetimes squeezing the last penny out of both the workers and the consumers in order to accumulate a large fortune so they can, at their deaths or before their deaths, give large gifts to charity in order to, in some degree at least, alleviate the suffering which the system through which they have accumulated their fortune has caused.

Every nation in the world is talking about peace, asking for peace, and still every nation in the world is arming to the limit. Our own country has passed neutrality laws and claims to be neutral in foreign troubles. We have hundreds of peace societies and congresses meeting annually in this country—and at the same time, our factories and munition makers are manufacturing and shipping millions of dollars' worth of war materials to other countries so that they may not only more efficiently murder each other, but that they may also put themselves in a position to threaten our peace because they have accumulated great stocks of war materials which were shipped from this country.

To justify this paradox, we are told that we must keep our munition manufacturers and other manufacturers of possible war materials in training so they can supply the war materials to our country in case it should be threatened by some foreign power.

Even we farmers work in paradoxes. We have some farm organizations which are strongly advocating control of all farm set ups by farmers as opposed to bureaucratic control and still they label any farmer who may accept a position under any of the federal agricultural set ups as a pay-roller, and try to read him out of the organization. Again, while opposing some bills with a large amount of bureaucratic control of agriculture, they are strongly in favor of other bills which give all power over setting the cost of farm products to the secretary of agriculture and his department.

We have other farmers who claim that they do not want to join any organization. That they are strong individualists and that all farmers should be individualists, and still these same farmers go to hearings and meetings and, at those hearings and meetings, claim to represent the unorganized farmer — the individual farmer.

We have farmers who are strong believers in farm organizations and in a fair return to the farmer for his work on his investment — but these same farmers are strongly opposed to the workers' organizations and are not willing that the worker should also have a fair return on his labor and on his time, forgetting that labor is the largest and best customer that the farmer has and that labor's buying power largely depends upon the farmer's ability to sell all the products of his farm at a fair price.

We also have labor leaders who are strong believers in a high wage for labor, who try to force farmers, who have no way to set the price on their products, to pay higher wages for farm labor than they can afford to pay based on the price of farm products. These labor leaders forget that every farmer who is forced to leave the farm becomes a competitor for the already too few jobs.

We need to take stock of ourselves. We need to think and to reason. We need to use not only our prejudices, but also to use our judgment, our reasoning power. If we want world peace, we must work toward world peace. If we want democracy, we must practice democracy at home.

There is only one way of assuring world peace and that is through a change in our economic system, through a change which will give each man a chance to exchange an honest day's labor for an honest day's labor of someone else, without permitting people who do not work to profit largely from the work of the other folks.

We cannot secure peace for ourselves, nor for the world by building great armies and great navies. Peace is not made that way. Most of the world's wars, as well as most of the revolutions, were started because some nation had a large army—and practically all the dictatorships were set up through the work and the use of oversized armies and navies.

If you have a large club, you will very likely try to use that club. If a nation has a large army, it is just natural that in time either it will use the army for foreign aggression or someone will use the army to overthrow the government and establish himself as a dictator. The army and navy are not good training grounds for democracy.

Security and democracy are not built on large standing armies or great navies. They are built upon the satisfaction, the contentment and happiness of the people. No nation will attack this nation or any other nation if its people are contented and happy, and if they have real reason to love their homes and their country.

The Farmers Union has, for a long time, pointed out the fallacy of many of the things which are being done, both in the name of bringing about world peace and of making better conditions for the common folks of this land. If we are to have economic security, and that in itself means political security and national security, we must remember that it can only be based upon a fair exchange between all groups and all classes of our citizenry. No one class can long be exploited for the benefit of others without affecting the well-being of all our people and the security of our country. The farmer must have his fair share of the national income, the laborer must have fair return for his labor and the same way with all other classes of our people.

Instead of accumulating immense fortunes on which they later must pay large inheritance taxes or give away to charity, our rich men should turn their attention to changing our system of trade and distribution so as to give employment to the greatest number of people possible at wages sufficient to enable them to buy the things that they need.

I am sure they would find far more pleasure in seeing satisfied citizens and well-fed, well-clothed healthy children than they do in giving their money, just before their deaths, to orphans' asylums, hospitals and other charities which are made necessary because of the system of legalized robbery which we call our system of economics, through the workings of which they have accumulated their millions.

One of the best ways to change this economic system is to develop, as much as possible, the cooperative idea. Change away from the idea of business or industry for profit, to the idea of business and industry for service. Develop our producers' cooperatives so that the producers of wealth, be it on the farms, in the mines, or in the factories, can receive for his product a fair share of the national income. Build our consumers' cooperatives so that the consumers can, in turn, buy their needs at a fair price without anyone making great profits out of the exchange of the goods.

In order to build sound cooperatives, we must educate our people and organize them so they can work together for the common good of all. I am strongly in favor of labor organizations, trade organizations and especially farm organizations. I believe by organizing each class, and then cooperating together for the common good of all, we can do more than in any other way to bring about peace and prosperity and make secure our democracy.

Through working of the economic system under which we live, we have developed an immense debt, both private and public. This debt is so large that it takes practically the entire productive income of the workers of this nation to pay only the interest on the debt, with nothing left to buy the necessities of life.

We are gradually coming to the place where we will not be able to pay the interest and still keep our people living. We are coming to the place where something must be done to lessen this burden of debt upon our people. Many times, in ancient times, this same condition existed and nearly always it has resulted in the downfall of the nation so burdened, and sometimes of the whole civilization. In biblical times, it gave rise to the provisions in the old law that every 30 years, all debts would be canceled and all property taken for debt was returned to the original owner of the property.

If we are to bring prosperity to this country, we must not wait too long before we do something about this debt situation. I am positive that the only reason Germany has been able to build such a large army, navy and air force has been because it, in effect, eliminated all domestic debts through the medium of inflation—and it repudiated most of its foreign debts so that it had more unencumbered real property at the beginning of Hitler's regime than almost any other country in the world.

I do not recommend repudiation of debts, nor unlimited inflation, but I do feel it is necessary for the welfare of not only the farmers but of this whole country, to compose all of our debts to an amount which the different classes and the country itself will be able to pay.

As far as our farmers are concerned, an estimate should be made of the reasonable productive value of all farm property and of the reasonable expectancy of income. Then, all farm debts should be composed to an amount commensurate with the farmers' ability to pay. The payments should be made on the basis of a percentage of the income of the farm. And, during the time when the farmer owes the debt, he should not be permitted to borrow any more money upon his land.

Our government ought to, and must, stop issuing tax-exempt interest-bearing bonds. The time will come when practically all of the property of the rich will be invested in these tax-exempt interest-bearing bonds, and the poor be left to pay all of the taxes through the medium of the sales tax and other levies on the needy.

Congress should take from the banks the power over our money supply which they now have. It should coin money and regulate the amount and value thereof. Either coin the gold hidden in the vault in Kentucky into money, or entirely forget about it.

If currency must be based on anything other than the credit of the country, then base it upon farm mortgages, or mortgages upon homes and upon warehoused commodities. In this way, there will be no danger of inflation beyond the needs of the country.

In good times, the farmers and others will pay off their debts on their homes, their property and their warehoused commodities, and reduce the amount of currency in circulation. In bad times, when they have to borrow, the borrowing will immediately increase the amount of currency in circulation and in that way, tend to increase the price of farm and other products, and enable the people to again pay off their debts.

We need a better understanding and closer cooperation between our farm organizations and labor organizations. We must realize that if a farmer is to have a good market for all his products, the laborer must receive a wage which will enable him to buy all the food, clothing and other necessities that he and his family need and to pay a fair price for them.

On the other hand, labor must realize that no industry, not even agriculture, can pay high wages if it is operating at a loss, and that in order to be able to pay fair wages to farm laborers and buy the products of labor in the factories, mines, etc., the farmers must also receive a fair price for their products.

Our agricultural and unemployment problems cannot be permanently solved simply by controlling production to effective demand, backed by the money to buy. Wheat at eight dollars a bushel or cotton at four cents a pound will not solve the farmer's problems if he is only permitted to raise a hundred bushels of wheat or a bale of cotton. Nor will two dollars per hour wage solve the labor problem if the laborer can only work five hours per week.

The real solution does not lie in a high per bushel or per pound price, nor in a high per hour wage alone. It can only be found in a fair annual income division between all classes of our citizens.

We must eliminate the monopolies which now exact such high tribute from both consumers and producers—that while the producer goes broke producing our necessities of life, millions are under-nourished and half-clothed because the price of these is so high that they cannot buy what they need to keep themselves in health and comfort.

What is the result of the monopoly control of our finance, trade and industry—and beginning control even of agriculture? Millions of men and women on relief who would like to work if only they could get a job. Factories, mines, lumber camps and other trade and industrial plants which should give employment to the millions on relief are silent and idle because over a third of our population does not have enough income to buy the products of industry. Thousands of our farmers are losing their farms every month and being turned out of the homes which it has taken them and their children a lifetime of toil and saving to build. The other millions are compelled to reduce productions of the necessities of life sorely needed by the under-nourished, poorly-clothed millions, because—after monopoly takes its toll—there is not enough money available to pay the farmer a decent living price for the products of his farm, nor for the needy to buy the food and fiber they need.

Let us all—rich, poor, farmer, laborer, financier, and industrialist—make a new year's resolution that we will try to correct the paradoxes of this age, that we will put human need and human happiness above desire for power, above the demands of greed. Let us counsel together how best we can repair this inefficient economic system of ours so as to bring work at fair wages to all who can and will work, so that, instead of building great fortunes in gold/silver bonds and other forms of property to the favored few at the expense of the many, it will bring happiness and contentment to all our people.

In asking for laws, let us ask for fair laws, consistent with the fundamental principles of Christianity and also of the Farmers Union, laws based on equity, justice and the application of the Golden Rule.

While demanding and working for needed remedial legislation, let us not forget that "in unity there is strength," and that "self-help is the best help." Let us build our Farmers Union larger and stronger in numbers and at the same time, educate our membership and our juniors in the real economics of production, distribution and financing—and above all, let us build and support all truly cooperative enterprises to the end that we may, as soon as possible, build up a new economic system based upon the principles of service and the greatest good to the greatest number, instead of the present system based upon large profits to the few and hunger and want to the many.

We need you—men, women and children—of the soil, to join in this great work of building a new understanding of man's duty to man. We need all of you to help us build this great organization and to spread far and wide its gospel of brotherly love.

We need you, workers in industry, to help bring about this change in our businesses and in our thinking so that we may each aid and supplement the other—and together form one great army fighting for the rights of the common people.

We need you: industrialists, financiers, politicians and all of you in important positions—to study history so as to find out for yourselves what the inevitable result of the concentration of wealth and of the control over means of production by a selfish few has always been. Russia is not under Dictator Stalin, nor Germany under Dictator Hitler, nor Italy under Mussolini by chance. It is not mere coincidence that there are a half-hundred minor modified dictatorships developing all over the world. It does not "just happen" that even in the so-called democracies, the people are compelled by economic pressure to surrender more and more of their liberties.

Large armies and navies are not being built by all the larger nations of the world because the majority of the people want to build and support them. All these are but the last efforts of a vicious economic system to perpetuate itself.

Unless we, the people of the United States, learn our lesson from history and take steps to safeguard the interests of all the people and give all a chance to enjoy the good things of this earth, which God has placed here for all his children, we too shall soon lose our civil liberties, as we have already, to a large extent, lost our economic liberties. Our civilization, through the building of huge armaments, is already forging the instruments for its destruction. Shall we wake up in time? Shall we reverse this seemingly inevitable march of destiny? The answer is in our hands.

If we organize the farmers, the laborers and all honest people of our land, and understandingly, courageously, start building for a better future, we are sure to win. Let's go.

Appendix III

From the memoirs of Jane Erickson (Clara Blake's sister), featuring Cora George and Frank Fox, my paternal grandparents:

I suppose all communities such as ours had their particularly outstanding "belle," a beautiful, gifted, popular "favorite." Ours, by the name of Cora George, surely could never be quite equaled for, as the saying goes, she "had everything." Beautiful, blonde curly hair, with deep blue eyes, a peaches-and-cream complexion and a figure to rival Evelyn Nesbitt Thaw or Lillian Russell (if these two immortals don't mind being mentioned in the same breath). She had long since finished her schooling and was living at home with her parents until her forthcoming marriage, (which seemed to be delayed for some reason year after year) to a "Beau Brummel" of a neighboring community—a dandy by the name of Frank Fox. Frank was looked on contemptuously by the young swains of our own community, probably because he was not of their own special homogeneity. I've called

Frank a "Beau Brummel," and he was just that. Always impeccably dressed, in the fanciest of attire, setting off to a tee his tightly curling hair and pretty blue eyes. The scuttlebutt was that he curled his hair, but I never believed it. However, he probably did manicure his fingernails, a habit not followed generally. In any event, he was anathema to the local rustics and they didn't hesitate to show it. They were one up in the situation, for Frank was deeply in love with Cora, and very jealous—and they didn't give a hoot!

The auction began—the boxes bringing anywhere from seventy-five cents up to two dollars, the top price. When it came time for Cora's box to (be) handed to the auctioneer, we were all a-tingle with the anticipation of what might happen. Frank very slyly kept silent at the initial bidding, so as not to arouse the suspicion that the box was Cora's. One dollar, one and a quarter, one fifty—then he came in. Two dollars. Needless to say, he wasn't going to have any one of those hoydens eat supper with his girl, and the bidding went on—and on—and on. When the fantastic amount of five dollars was reached, the excitement in the room was (at) a fever pitch. Cora was blushing furiously, and Frank had lost the good-natured smile he usually wore—his demeanor showing a steely determination. It was as though the air in the room had been charged with some high explosive that might detonate at any minute, all of us sharing in the desperate game. When finally the bidding had mounted to the stupendous figure of seven dollars and fifty cents, the auctioneer, deciding the suspense had gone on long enough, ended the competition abruptly by a "Going—going—gone! Sold to Frank Fox!"

And the great question was settled. Each side got what it wanted—Frank to eat with his Cora, and the yokels making him pay what was then considered a fantastic price for the privilege. In fairness to Frank, he married his sweetheart soon thereafter, and must have enjoyed, without any outside bedevilment, her good cooking, for many years to come.

Appendix IV

From Chapter 7, "Unhappy Memories," excerpted from *My Autobiography*, by Genevieve Elizabeth Fox (1930):

The narrowest escape I ever had was when I ran into a ditch. Don, my brother, had just bought a secondhand car, a Ford. He painted it black and trimmed it with red paint. He wouldn't let me drive it because I didn't know how, although I thought I did.

One day, Bill and Don went to Abilene. A girlfriend (of) mine from Kansas City was visiting at her cousin's, Mrs. Mall. I called up Arlene and she came over. She knew how to drive better than I. We went upstairs and got the car keys, started the car, went out after Julia and then went to Oak Hill. We took turns driving the car. It happened to be my turn, so I drove home. When we came to the corner by the Rose Meron Cemetery, I had planned on going straight on, but Arlene said to turn east and Julia said south. I was so confused that I turned too late and pleased them both by going in between. We landed in a deep ditch. Luckily, we did not turn over. We all (were) so frightened, we didn't know what to do. We laughed and cried both at the same time.

The car was pretty well tipped. We tried to push it out but we couldn't move it a fraction of an inch. We went up to a nearby house and Julia called my folks and said that we ran into a little ditch, but it didn't hurt anything. The man went down and tried to pull it out with a team of horses, but he couldn't. Two cars came along and they couldn't, and then a tractor came along and with the help of three men, they got it out. The radius rod was broken. Just as we got it out, Don and Bill came. My heart was surely beating fast. He (Don) didn't say much but he sure was mad. He said that it would be the last time I would get to drive his car.

Julia went home with me. Dad didn't say much; he laughed because Don was so mad. Don often laughs over it now.

After that, every once in a while, Arlene and I would take a fingernail file and start the car, but we never tried to turn a corner after we were past it. I shall always remember the old Ford.